Get Started
In Danish

Teach Yourself®

Get started In Danish

Dorte Al-Gailani

Advisory editor
Beth Beemer

First published in Great Britain in 2015 by John Murray Learning. An Hachette UK company.

British Library Cataloguing in Publication Data: a catalogue record for this title is available from the British Library.

Library of Congress Catalog Card Number: on file.

9781444798630

4

The publisher has used its best endeavours to ensure that any website addresses referred to in this book are correct and active at the time of going to press. However, the publisher and the author have no responsibility for the websites and can make no guarantee that a site will remain live or that the content will remain relevant, decent or appropriate.

The publisher has made every effort to mark as such all words which it believes to be trademarks. The publisher should also like to make it clear that the presence of a word in the book, whether marked or unmarked, in no way affects its legal status as a trademark.

Every reasonable effort has been made by the publisher to trace the copyright holders of material in this book. Any errors or omissions should be notified in writing to the publisher, who will endeavour to rectify the situation for any reprints and future editions.

Cover image ©

Typeset by Cenveo® Publisher Services.

Printed and bound in Great Britain by CPI Group (UK) Ltd, Croydon CR0 4YY

John Murray Learning policy is to use papers that are natural, renewable and recyclable products and made from wood grown in sustainable forests. The logging and manufacturing processes are expected to conform to the environmental regulations of the country of origin.

Carmelite House
50 Victoria Embankment
London EC4Y 0DZ
www.hodder.co.uk

Contents

About the author

I grew up in the western part of Jutland in Denmark and completed my masters degree in history at Syddansk Universitet before moving to Scotland. I have always had a great interest in languages and having attended language classes myself in both European and non-European languages in a huge variety of settings, I decided to try things from the other side. I gained TEFL certification and eventually found myself teaching Danish at Glasgow University and as a private tutor. After years of doing this to a range of fantastic students I am still amazed by the enthusiasm shown for learning my native language with its sometimes unfamiliar sounds and flat intonation and I hope to continue enjoying it for many years to come.

Dorte Al-Gailani

How this book works

What you will learn identifies what you should be able to do in Danish by the end of the unit.

Culture points present cultural aspects related to the themes in the units, introducing key words and phrases and including follow-up questions.

Vocabulary builder introduces key unit vocabulary grouped by theme and conversation, accompanied by audio. By learning the words and listening to them, your progress in learning contemporary Danish will be swift.

Conversations and dialogues are recorded dialogues that you can listen to and practise, beginning with a narrative that helps you understand what you are going to hear, with a focusing question and follow-up activities.

Language discovery draws your attention to key language points in the conversations and to rules of grammar and pronunciation. Read the notes and look at the conversations to see how the language is used in practice.

Practice offers a variety of exercises, including speaking opportunities, to give you a chance to see and use words and phrases in their context.

Speaking and listening offer practice in speaking and understanding Danish through exercises that let you use what you have learned in previous units.

Reading and writing provide practice in reading everyday items and contain mostly vocabulary from the unit. Try to get the main point of the text before you answer the follow-up questions.

Test yourself helps you assess what you have learned. You learn more by doing the tests without looking at the text, and only when you have done them check if your answers are the correct ones (do not cheat!).

Self check lets you see what you can do after having completed each unit.

To help you through the course, a system of icons indicates the actions to take.

 Listen to audio

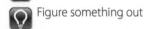 Speak Danish out loud

 Figure something out

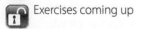 Culture tip

 Exercises coming up

 Reading passage

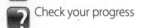 Write and make notes

 Check your progress

Here are some further resources in the book for you to consult:

Useful expressions list commonly used everyday phrases

Review units sum up what you have learned in the previous units. There are three reviews: after Unit 3, after Unit 6, and after Unit 10. If you master all questions in the review unit, go ahead; if not, go back and refresh your knowledge.

The **Answer key** helps you check your progress by including answers to the activities both in the text units and the review units.

Learn to learn

The discovery method

This book incorporates the discovery method of learning. You will be encouraged throughout the course to engage your mind and figure out the meaning for yourself, through identifying patterns and understanding grammatical concepts, noticing words that are similar to English, and more. As a result of your efforts, you will be able to retain what you have learned, use it with confidence, and continue to learn the language on your own after you have finished this book.

Everyone can succeed in learning a language – the key is to know how to learn it. Learning is more than just reading or memorizing grammar and vocabulary. It is about being an active learner, learning in real contexts, and using in different situations what you have learned. If you figure something out for yourself, you are more likely to understand it, and when you use what you have learned, you are more likely to remember it.

As many of the essential details, such as grammar rules, are introduced through the discovery method, you will have more fun while learning. The language will soon start to make sense and you will be relying on your own intuition to construct original sentences independently, not just by listening and repeating.

Happy learning!

Pronunciation guide

Danish is not the easiest of languages to get used to, but once you are able to understand some of the quirks you are well on your way.

One of the main problems is that Danes have a habit of what seems to be mumbling and swallowing quite a lot of sounds, rather than pronouncing every syllable clearly. This, combined with the fact that Danish is a very flat language with limited intonation, can make it hard when you first start out to recognize individual words in a sentence. It will all come with practice! Grab every opportunity you can to listen to Danish. Danish films and TV programmes are excellent for this as they will normally have English subtitles and you therefore have a chance to listen out for specific words that you know. The internet is also a great source of help.

Listening to a lot of Danish will also make it easier for you to pronounce it as you will recognize more subtleties in the language. When you visit Denmark speak as much Danish as possible, even though the Danes are likely to speak English to you! If you happen to know anybody Danish where you live or work, ask them to speak Danish to you and to help with the pronunciation. If you have the facility on your phone or computer try to record yourself speaking Danish and then play it back, so you can hear your own pronunciation and make adjustments.

When doing the listening exercises in this book, try to listen to them first without looking at the written text to sharpen your ability to understand spoken Danish.

0.01 Alphabet

The Danish alphabet has 29 letters.

Aa	**Ii**
Bb	**Jj**
Cc	**Kk**
Dd	**Ll**
Ee	**Mm**
Ff	**Nn**
Gg	**Oo**
Hh	**Pp**

Qq	**Rr**
Ss	**Yy**
Tt	**Zz**
Uu	**Ææ**
Vv	**Øø**
Ww	**Åå**
Xx	

 0.02 The last three letters are vowels and **y** is also a vowel in Danish, meaning that Danish has nine vowels altogether: **a**, **e**, **i**, **o**, **u**, **y**, **æ**, **ø**, **å**.

The letters **c**, **q**, **w**, **x**, **z** are only used in words imported from other languages and are not common.

 ## 0.03 Vowels

Letter	Pronunciation/varieties	Examples
a	Short, similar to the English 'a' in *cat*	**kat, sandt**
	Long, same sound as the short 'a' but drawn out	**gade, male**
e	Short, like in the English *pen*	**besøg**
	Long, same sound as the short 'e' but drawn out	**mel**
	At the end of a word 'e' is often half swallowed. It is not silent, but not pronounced clearly either, so it becomes closer to an 'o' sound. A lot of verbs end in 'e' as do quite a few Danish names.	**Ingen, hoppe, Pernille**
i	Short, like in the English *bin*	**minut**
	Long, similar to the English 'ee' in *see* or 'ea' in *sea*	**ride, dine**
o	Short, like the English 'o' in *gone*	**flot**
	Long, close to the English 'oa' in *coal*	**hoste**
u	Short, close to the English 'u' in *put*	**du, kuld**
	Long, similar to the English 'oo' in *boot*	**frue, regnbue**
y	Short, pronounced like 'ø' (see below)	**lykke**
	Long, there is no English equivalent. You need to purse your lips to say it. The sound is similar to the German 'ü', or the French 'u' in 'tu'.	**ymer, lyve**
æ	A more open form of 'e', quite close to the 'ai' sound in *pain*	**Æble, læse**
ø	You need rounded lips like for 'o'. Similar to the German 'ö' or the French 'eu'.	**købe**
å	Open sounding 'o'	**Blå, kåbe**

0.04 Certain vowel–consonant combinations also create a diphthong.

-og/-ov	Similar to the 'ow' in *crow*	**og, doven**
øj	Similar to the 'oy' in *boy*	**høj, støj**
-ej/-aj /-eg*	Similar to the 'y' in *my*	**nej, meget**
-av/af- **	Like the 'ow' in *cow*	**København, afstand**

 ## 0.05 Consonants

A lot of the consonants in Danish are the same as in English. The main things to notice are:

▶ hardly any consonants are voiced in Danish so, for example, there is only one 's' sound, whereas English has more (think about the difference between the 's' in *sun* which is not voiced and the 's' in *please* which is voiced)

▶ pay particular attention to **d**, **t**, **g** and **j**.

Letter	Pronunciation/varieties	Examples
b	As in English	**banan** (*banana*)
	Gliding, like an English 'w' (very rare)	**peber** (*pepper*)
c	As in English it can be 's' sound or 'k' sound	**cykel** (*bike*), **Canada**
d	Hard 'd'	**dansker** (*Dane*), **arbejde** (*work*)
	Silent 'd' (usually in the combinations **-ld**, **-nd**, **-dt**, **-ds**, **-rd**)	**kold** (*cold*), **kende** (*know*), **land** (*country*), **rødt** (*red*), **bord** (*table*)
	Soft 'd', this is a sound that can cause problems when learning Danish. Many people hear it as an 'l' sound, but it is not! When doing an 'l' sound the tongue goes behind the top front teeth; when doing a soft 'd' the tongue goes behind the bottom front teeth.	**sød** (*sweet*), **fløde** (*cream*), **sidde** (*sit*)
f	As in English	**fisk** (*fish*)
g	Hard	**god** (*good*), **grim** (*ugly*)
	Soft, at the end of a syllable, almost silent	**pige** (*girl*), **bog** (*book*)

---

* This is also the case for these three words: **mig**, **dig**, **sig**.

* * The preposition 'af' does not follow this pattern, it is simply pronounced as 'a'.

h	Always pronounced before a vowel	**hus** (*house*)
	Never pronounced before a consonant	**hvem** (*who*), **hvor** (*where*)
j	Close to the English 'y'	**ja** (*yes*)
k	Always pronounced, even in a **kn-** combination	**kniv** (*knife*)
	A double 'kk' is pronounced like 'gg'	**ikke** (*not*), **sukker** (*sugar*)
l	As in English	**lærer** (*teacher*)
m	As in English	**mælk** (*milk*)
n	As in English	**navn** (*name*)
p	As in English	**plet** (*stain*), **politi** (*police*)
	A double 'pp' is pronounced like 'bb'	**Jeppe** (*boy's name*)
q	Pronounced like 'k'	**quiz**
r	Pronounced at the back of the throat.	**ræv** (*fox*), **rød** (*red*)
s	Never voiced, so like the 's' sound in *sun* (Remember that an 's' on its own cannot give a 'sh' sound.)	**sur** (*sour*), **sild** (*herring*)
t	In the beginning of a word generally pronounced like 't' in the English *try*	**tivoli**, **torsk** (*cod*)
	In the combination **-te** at the end of a word the 't' is often pronounced like a hard 'd'	**Dorte** (*girl's name*), **vente** (*wait*)
	Silent in **det** and sometimes **at**	**det** (*it*)
	Double 'tt' is pronounced like 'dd'	**hætte** (*hood*)
	In a past participle 't' has the same sound as the soft 'd'	**gået** (*gone*), **vasket** (*washed*)
v	Usually silent after 'l'	**gulv** (*floor*), **selv** (*self*)
w	Pronounced like 'v'	**weekend**
x	Pronounced like 's'	**xylofon**
z	Pronounced like 's'	**zebra**

 0.06 Most words have the stress on the first syllable, but there are exceptions, such as:

▶ words starting with **be-**, or **er-** (**berette**, **erhverv**)
▶ words borrowed from French which normally keep the French stress on the last syllable (**universitetet, station**, **information**).

The intonation of Danish is generally quite flat, often with a tendency to go down at the end of a sentence. In spoken language, words often appear to merge together with very little gap between them and the endings of words are regularly cut short.

Goddag/Farvel

Hello/Goodbye

In this unit you will learn how to:
▶ *say hello and goodbye.*
▶ *introduce yourself.*
▶ *say where you come from and where you live.*
▶ *use verbs in the present tense.*
▶ *use personal pronouns.*
▶ *ask simple questions.*

CEFR: (A1) *Can introduce yourself and others and can ask and answer questions about personal details such as where you live. Can make an introduction and use basic greeting and leave-taking expressions.*

 Greetings

The Danes are generally very informal. When Danes meet friends or family they tend to give each other a hug, or in less familiar circumstances such as at business meetings they will shake hands.

The most common expressions for greeting people are **hej**, **dav**, or **goddag** (slightly more formal). Depending on the time of day you can also use **godmorgen**, **godformiddag**, **godeftermiddag**, **godaften** or **godnat**.

When leaving people tend to use **hej-hej**, **vi ses** or **farvel**.

1 What do you think these expressions translate as?

> **Godmorgen, Goddag, Godeftermiddag, Godaften, Godnat**

It is worth noting that **godmorgen** is not used after 10 a.m. Between 10 and 12 you should use **godformiddag** or **goddag**, otherwise you are giving the impression you just got out of bed. **Formiddag** literally means *before noon*.

(Or you can always go for the easy option and use **hej**!)

Vocabulary builder

01.01 **Look at the words and phrases and complete the missing English expressions. Then listen and try to imitate the pronunciation of the speakers.**

GREETINGS

Hej	_____
Dav	*Hello/Hi*
Goddag	*Good day* (more formal)
Hvad så?	*What's up?*
Hvordan går det?	*How is it going?/How are you doing?*
Hvordan står det til?	*How are things?*
Vi ses	_____
Farvel	*Goodbye* (more formal)

PERSONAL INFORMATION

Jeg hedder ...	*I am called ... (My name is ...)*
Jeg bor i ...	*I live in ...*
Jeg kommer fra ...	*I come from ...*
Jeg er ...	*I am ...* (followed by your nationality)

NEW WORDS AND EXPRESSIONS

Look at the words and expressions that are used in the following conversation. Note their meanings.

at sidde	*to sit*
Det er fint	*That is fine*
Hvor skal du hen?	*Where are you going?*
at arbejde	*to work*
at lave	*to do*
en læge (-r)	*doctor*
en lærer (-e)	*teacher*
at undervise	*to teach*
Hvor spændende	*How exciting*
holde ferie	*going on holiday*
at rejse	*to travel*
at besøge	*to visit*
Hyggeligt at møde dig	*It was nice to meet you*

Conversation 1

 01.02 *Niels is getting on the train from Copenhagen to Aalborg. There is an empty seat next to Maria and he asks if he can sit there.*

1   Listen to the conversation. Where is Maria going?

Niels	Dav, må jeg sidde her?
Maria	Ja, det er fint.
Niels	Jeg skal til Aalborg, hvor skal du hen?
Maria	Jeg skal kun til Roskilde.
Niels	Jeg hedder Niels. Jeg arbejder i Aalborg.
Maria	Hvad laver du?
Niels	Jeg er læge. Hvad laver du?
Maria	Jeg er lærer. Jeg underviser i spansk. Jeg kommer fra Spanien.
Niels	Hvor spændende! Jeg holder ferie i Spanien om sommeren, men jeg er dansker. Hvad hedder du?
Maria	Jeg hedder Maria. Jeg kommer fra Barcelona, men nu bor jeg i Roskilde.
Niels	Jeg bor i Aalborg, men jeg rejser ofte til København og besøger min familie.
Maria	Nu er vi i Roskilde. Det var hyggeligt at møde dig.
Niels	Farvel.
Maria	Hej hej!

2   Read the conversation again and answer these questions.

  a Where is Niels going?
  b What is Niels's job?
  c What is Maria's job?
  d Where is Maria from?
  e Where does Maria live now?

Language discovery

1 Look at the dialogue. How do you do the following?
   a Ask a person's name.
   b Ask about a person's job.

2 How do you translate the following?
   a I am a doctor.
   b I am a teacher.

3 Do you notice any difference between the English and the Danish sentence when describing a profession?

4 How are the following verbs translated into Danish?
   a live
   b come
   c visit
   d teach

5 What do you notice about the endings of those verbs in the text?

6 How did Maria say where she was from? What is the word for a Danish person?

1 NATIONALITIES AND LANGUAGES

In Danish as a very general rule nationalities usually end in **-er**, like **dansker**. There are, however, several exceptions to that rule! The language spoken ends in **-sk**, like **dansk**.

Here is short list of a few countries.

Country	Nationality	Language
Danmark	dansker	dansk
England	englænder	engelsk
Irland	irer	(irsk)
Amerika	amerikaner	(amerikansk)
Skotland	skotte	(skotsk)
Wales	waliser	walisisk
Tyskland (*Germany*)	tysker	tysk
Spanien (*Spain*)	spanier	spansk
Frankrig (*France*)	franskmand	fransk
Sverige (*Sweden*)	svensker	svensk
Norge (*Norway*)	nordmand	norsk

Notice that the adjectives are not capitalized, for example, **dansker**, **spanier**, **dansk**, **spansk**:

Jeg kommer fra Danmark, jeg er dansker og jeg taler dansk.
Jeg hedder Simon, jeg er skotte men jeg bor i England. Jeg taler engelsk og dansk og lidt fransk.

 Ulla er dansker. Uffe er nordmand. De taler dansk og norsk.

Can you spot any nationalities that don't follow the -er rule?

2 PERSONAL PRONOUNS

Personal pronouns are the words we use instead of a name or a noun to avoid repetition. The personal pronoun is different depending on whether it is the subject of the sentence or not, as in English (*I* or *me*).

The following table gives the personal pronouns in Danish along with the English equivalent.

jeg	*I*	**mig**	*me*
du	*you* (singular)	**dig**	*you* (singular)
han	*he*	**ham**	*him*
hun	*she*	**hende**	*her*
den/det	*it*	**den/det**	*it*
vi	*we*	**os**	*us*
I	*you* (plural)	**jer**	*you* (plural)
de	*they*	**dem**	*them*

Danish also has a very formal/polite version of **du** and **I** which is **De** (with a capital letter).

This form is hardly ever used nowadays, so unless you find yourself in the company of the royal family you are unlikely to need it. Obviously if somebody does use **De** when speaking to you, you should reply with **De** as well.

Here are some examples of personal pronouns used with the verb *at møde* (*to meet*).

Vi møder ham	*We meet him*
Han møder hende	*He meets her*
De møder mig	*They meet me*
Hun møder dem	*She meets them*

3 VERBS IN THE PRESENT TENSE

In Danish all verbs in the infinitive end in a vowel: **at tale** (*to speak*), **at besøge** (*to visit*), **at bo** (*to live*). This is the form you will find in a dictionary.

In the present tense they end in **-r** (**taler**, **besøger**, **bor**).

Jeg taler dansk	*I speak Danish*
Du taler engelsk	*You speak English*
Han taler fransk	*He speaks French*
Hun taler spansk	*She speaks Spanish*
Vi taler dansk	*We speak Danish*
I taler tysk	*You speak German*
De taler svensk	*They speak Swedish*

Jeg hedder Peter, jeg bor i Skotland, men jeg kommer fra England. Jeg er lærer og jeg taler engelsk.

My name is Peter, I live in Scotland but I come from England. I am a teacher and I speak English.

> There is only one form of the present tense in Danish as opposed to English. In Danish there is no difference between *I am speaking Danish* and *I speak Danish*, both forms would translate as **Jeg taler dansk**.

4 QUESTIONS IN DANISH

These are the basic question words in Danish:

hvor	*where*	**Hvor bor du?**	*Where do you live?*
hvad	*what*	**Hvad laver du?**	*What do you do?*
hvem	*who*	**Hvem er det?**	*Who is that?*
hvornår	*when*	**Hvornår kommer du?**	*When are you coming?*
hvordan	*how*	**Hvordan går det?**	*How are you doing?*
hvorfor	*why*	**Hvorfor griner du?**	*Why are you laughing?*
hvilken/hvilket	*which*	**Hvilken bog er bedst?**	*Which book is best?*
hvor gammel	*how old*	**Hvor gammel er du?**	*How old are you?*

🔓 Practice

1 Match the Danish to the English translation.

a	Jeg møder dig	**1**	You (singular) meet us
b	Han møder mig	**2**	They meet him
c	Du møder os	**3**	He meets me
d	Hun møder jer	**4**	I meet you
e	I møder dem	**5**	We meet her
f	De møder ham	**6**	You (plural) meet them
g	Vi møder hende	**7**	She meets you

2 Translate the following into Danish.

    a He lives in Boston.
    b I come from England.
    c They visit Niels.
    d You speak Danish.

3 Answer these questions with your own information.

    a Hvad hedder du?
    b Hvor bor du?
    c Hvor kommer du fra?
    d Hvad laver du?

NEW WORDS AND EXPRESSIONS

Er du glad for arbejdet?	*Do you like your job?*
stadig	*still*
tit	*often*
et sted (-er)	*place*
at have tid	*to have time*
senere	*later*

Conversation 2

 01.03 *Mette and Sofie have not seen each other for a long time but they run into each other at the gym.*

1 What are their jobs?

Sofie	Hej Mette. Hvordan går det?
Mette	Det går fint, tak. Hvad med dig?
Sofie	Jo tak, det går udmærket. Hvor arbejder du nu?
Mette	Jeg arbejder for Mærsk som ingeniør. Er du stadig arkitekt?
Sofie	Ja, det er jeg; nu arbejder jeg i København.
Mette	Er du glad for arbejdet?
Sofie	Ja, det er et fint sted at arbejde. Kommer du tit her i motionscenteret?
Mette	Kun når jeg har tid.
Sofie	Har du tid til en kop kaffe senere?
Mette	Ja, det ville være hyggeligt.
Sofie	Vi ses senere.
Mette	Hej hej.

2 Read or listen to the conversation again and answer these questions.

  a Where does Sofie work?
  b Is she enjoying her job?
  c How often does Mette go to the gym?
  d What are they doing later?

Speaking

01.04 Complete this conversation with Morten.

Morten	Hej
You	*(Hi)*
Morten	Jeg hedder Morten. Hvad hedder du?
You	*(My name is ..., where do you live?)*
Morten	Jeg bor i Odense. Hvor bor du?
You	*(I live in ...)*

Reading

The following text is a summary of the first conversation in this unit.

Maria og Niels sidder i toget fra København. Niels fortæller at han er læge og han bor i Aalborg. Maria er lærer, hun underviser i spansk. Hun kommer fra Spanien, men bor i Danmark nu. Niels holder tit ferie i Spanien om sommeren. I Roskilde siger Maria farvel til Niels.

Based on the text answer the following questions in Danish.

   a Hvad laver Maria?
   b Hvor bor Maria?
   c Hvor kommer Maria fra?
   d Hvad laver Niels?
   e Hvor holder Niels ferie?

Writing

1 **Write a paragraph in Danish about yourself (your name, where you live, your nationality, any languages you speak, what you do).**

2 **Put the words in the right order to make a sentence in Danish.**

   a i Jeg København arkitekt er
   b kop tid du til en kaffe Har?
   c Jeg Danmark hedder kommer jeg fra og Morten

Test yourself

1 What would you say in the following situations?

  a To your colleagues when you arrive at work in the morning

  b When you meet a friend

  c When you leave a business meeting

  d To your family when you go to bed

2 How do you ask the following questions?

  a What is your name?

  b Where do you live?

  c What do you do?

3 Insert the correct pronoun.

  a Han møder (*her*)

  b (*We*) møder dig

  c Du møder (*him*)

  d (*They*) møder hende

  e (*I*) møder jer

4 Translate the following into Danish.

  a She is a doctor.

  b We come from Spain.

  c My name is Peter and I am English.

  d He speaks English, Danish and French.

  e How is it going?

  f Maria meets us in the train.

SELF CHECK

I CAN ...
... say *hello* and *goodbye*.
... introduce myself.
... say where I come from and where I live.
... use verbs in the present tense.
... use personal pronouns.
... ask questions.

Min familie

My family

In this unit you will learn how to:
▶ *describe your family.*
▶ *count to 20.*
▶ *use nouns in the singular and plural.*

CEFR: (A1) *Can recognize familiar words and phrases concerning self and family. Can handle numbers, quantities, cost and time. Can write short, simple notes.*

 Relatives

Danish for *mother* and *father* is **mor** and **far**; they are your **forældre** (*parents*). **En bror** (*brother*) and **en søster** (*sister*) are your **søskende** (*siblings*). In Danish quite often the words you use for relatives indicate if you are related on your mother's side or your father's, for example, your maternal grandmother is **mormor**, where as your paternal grandmother is **farmor**. Your father's sister is **faster**, but your mother's sister is **moster**. The people you are related to by marriage will have 'sviger' in front, so your parents-in-law are **svigermor** and **svigerfar**. Sister-in-law is **svigerinde** and brother-in-law is **svoger**.

If your mother's father is **morfar**, what do you think your father's father is?

Vocabulary builder

02.01 **Look at the words and phrases and complete the missing English expressions. Then listen and try to imitate the pronunciation of the speakers.**

MORE RELATIVES

en søn (ner)	_____
en datter (døtre)	*daughter*
et barn (børn)	*child*
et barnebarn	_____
en fætter (re)	*male cousin*
en kusine (r)	*female cousin*
gift med	*married to*
en mand (mænd)	*husband/man*
en kone (r)	*wife*
en kæreste (r)	*boyfriend/girlfriend*
en partner (e)	_____

NEW WORDS AND EXPRESSIONS

Look at the words and expressions that are used in the following conversation. Note their meanings.

stor	*big*
gammel	*old*
et billede (r)	*picture*
et hus (e)	*house*
også	*too*
syv	*seven*
ni	*nine*
tolv	*twelve*
femten	*fifteen*
seksten	*sixteen*

Conversation 1

 02.02 *Sonja is looking at family photos with her granddaughter Emilie.*

1 Listen to the dialogue. What is Emilie's sister called?

Sonja	Her er et billede af din mor, da hun var lille. Hun sidder sammen med sin bror – onkel Jan. Han er min søn.
Emilie	Jeg har ikke nogen bror, jeg har kun en storesøster!
Sonja	Her er din mor igen, sammen med din far og din søster Sofie; og her er din mor med alle fætrene og kusinerne. Hun har syv fætre og ni kusiner. Hvor mange fætre og kusiner har du, Emilie?
Emilie	Jeg har en kusine, Emma, men jeg har 1-2-3-4 fætre. Hvad med dig mormor, hvor mange har du?
Sonja	Hmm, lad mig se. Jeg har tolv fætre og seksten, nej femten kusiner.
Emilie	Det er mange.
Sonja	Ja, vi er en stor familie. Her er et gammelt billede af mig og morfar, og her er min bror og hans kone.
Emilie	Hvad hedder de?
Sonja	De hedder Jens og Lise. De bor i Horsens og de har en søn og en datter. Sønnen hedder Claus og han har et barn. Datteren hedder Rikke, hun har to sønner .
Emilie	Mormor, jeg kan godt lide at se billeder.
Sonja	Ja, det er hyggeligt.

2 Read the conversation again and answer these questions.
   a Does Emilie have a brother?
   b How many cousins does Emilie have?
   c What is the name of Sonja's brother?
   d How many children and grandchildren does Sonja's brother have?

Hyggeligt or **hygge** is a word the Danes are proud of. In many situations it will translate into English as *lovely, cosy* or *nice*, but it does in fact indicate more than just that. **Hygge** is an atmosphere and a feeling as well as being something nice, and it is an essential part of how the Danes characterize themselves.

3 Listen to the dialogue again and write down any numbers that you pick out.

4 Find all versions of the words for *female cousin* **and for** *son* **in the text. What do you think each version means?**

Language discovery

1 NUMBERS IN DANISH

02.03 **Here are the numbers 1–20. Listen and try to repeat.**

1	**en**	11	**elleve**
2	**to**	12	**tolv**
3	**tre**	13	**tretten**
4	**fire**	14	**fjorten**
5	**fem**	15	**femten**
6	**seks**	16	**seksten**
7	**syv**	17	**sytten**
8	**otte**	18	**atten**
9	**ni**	19	**nitten**
10	**ti**	20	**tyve**

2 NOUNS IN THE DEFINITE AND INDEFINITE FORMS

A house is an example of a noun in the indefinite form; *the house* is a noun in the definite form.

There are two kinds of nouns in Danish.

1 Common gender that have **en** in front (**en mand**, **en kone**) in the indefinite form.

2 Neuter that have **et** in front (**et hus**, **et barn**) in the indefinite form.

Unfortunately it is hard to make specific rules for which should have **en** and which should have **et**. Approximately 75 per cent of nouns have **en** in front while 25 per cent have **et**, so if you have to make a guess you should probably opt for **en**.

Dictionaries normally indicate if it is one or the other, as does this book in all vocabulary lists. In a dictionary it often looks like this **mand (-n)**, which means it would be **en mand**.

En and **et** are also used to create the definite form of any noun. You simply move it from the front and place it at the end of the noun, so for example **en mand** (*a man*) becomes **manden** (*the man*), or **et hus** (*a house*) becomes **huset** (*the house*).

Here are a few more examples.

en datter	*a daughter*	**datteren**	*the daughter*
en familie	*a family*	**familien**	*the family*
et barn	*a child*	**barnet**	*the child*

Look at the dialogue again and find at least three words with **en** and one word with **et**. What would they be in the definite form?

Remember that if the noun ends in an **e** you would normally just add **n** or **t** (**en kusine** becomes **kusinen**) unless the 'e' is stressed in which case you need to retain both e's (**en ide** becomes **ideen**). If the noun ends in a consonant it will double up if it is preceded by a short vowel (**en søn** becomes **sønnen**).

3 PLURAL FORMS OF NOUNS

There are three types of plural in the indefinite form.

▶ Add **r** or **er** to the indefinite form of the word (**en kusine** becomes **kusiner**, **en læge** becomes **læger**).

▶ Add **e** to the indefinite form of the word (**et hus** becomes **huse**, **en dansker** becomes **danskere**).

▶ No ending, but sometimes a change of vowel (**en mand** becomes **mænd**, **en fisk** becomes **fisk**).

A dictionary should indicate what type of plural a noun takes.

You saw before that the singular definite form is created by adding to the end of the word. With that in mind what do you think the following words mean: **husene**, **lægerne**, **mændene**?

What would you add to a noun in plural to make it the definite form?

The definite form of a plural noun is normally created by adding **ne** or **ene** to the indefinite plural form.

borde becomes **bordene** (*tables* becomes *the tables*)

sønner becomes **sønnerne** (*sons* becomes *the sons*)

børn becomes **børnene** (*children* becomes *the children*)

Look at the conversation again and find three words in the plural. Are they in the definite or indefinite form?

Practice

1 Put these numbers in order, starting with the smallest.

elleve, otte, fem, sytten, fjorten, fire, to, tolv, seksten, ti

Use these numbers to help you count to 20.

2 Fill in the gaps with the indefinite and definite forms of the nouns given.

Indefinite	Definite
et bord	
en læge	
	englænderen
et hus	
	konen
et billede	
en søster	

3 Complete the sentences.

  a Peter har 3 _____ (*sons*).

  b Emilie og Emma er _____ (*cousins*).

  c Der bor 5.6 millioner _____ (*Danes*) i Danmark.

  d Der er 5 _____ (*men*) i huset.

4 What is the definite plural form of the following words?

  a koner

  b familier

  c børn

  d fætre

Listening and speaking

02.04 Listen to Simon introducing his family.

Hej! Jeg hedder Simon. Jeg er gift med Charlotte, og vi har to børn, Anne og Frederik. Anne er syv år og Frederik er ti. Vi bor i Horsens. Charlotte kommer fra England, men hun har boet i Danmark i sytten år.

Mine forældre hedder Bente og Vagn, de bor i Allerød. Børnene elsker at besøge deres farmor og farfar.

Vi er en stor familie. Jeg har to brødre, Lars og Jens. Lars er gift med Sanne og de har tre børn. Jens er gift med Lotte og de har også tre børn. Alt i alt har min mor og far otte børnebørn.

Jeg har også fire kusiner og syv fætre.

Answer the following questions in Danish.

  a Hvor gammel er Anne?

  b Hvor bor Bente og Vagn?

  c Hvor kommer Charlotte fra?

  d Hvad hedder Simons brødre?

  e Hvor mange børnebørn har Bente og Vagn?

 Reading

02.05 Read and listen to the text then fill out the family tree.

Søren er gift med Mette. De har to børn, Laura og Emil og de bor i et hus i Hvidovre. Sørens forældre hedder Jørgen og Merete, de bor også i et hus i Hvidovre. Søren har også en bror som hedder Peter, og en søster som hedder Jette. Jette er kæreste med Jonas. Mettes forældre hedder Niels og Lis, de bor i Odense. Mette har ingen søskende, Niels og Lis har kun et barn.

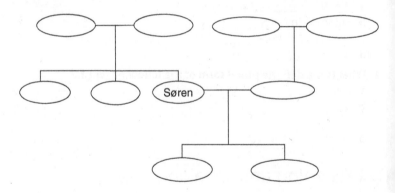

Writing

Write an email to a friend introducing your family.

When sending an email to a friend you can start it with **Hej ...** In a slightly more formal setting if you know the name of the person you are emailing you would normally use **Kære ...** If you are writing to, for example, the bank and there is no named contact, just use **Til ...**

When signing off the email, the formal phrase to use would be **Venlig hilsen**. If it is for family or friends use **Kærlig hilsen** or **Knus**.

Test yourself

1 Write the following numbers as figures.
   a fire
   b seksten
   c tolv
   d syv
   e nitten
   f otte
   g elleve

2 Translate the following sentences.
   a Sophie is nine years old.
   b Kirsten and Caroline are cousins.
   c We have five grandchildren.
   d I am married to Jill.

3 Complete the table.

Singular indefinite	Singular definite	Plural indefinite	Plural definite
en kone			
		borde	
	kusinen		
		sønner	
			mændene
et barn			

SELF CHECK

I CAN ...

○ ... describe my family.

○ ... count to 20.

○ ... use nouns in the singular and plural.

3 *På restaurant og cafe*

Eating out

In this unit, you will learn how to:
▶ *read a menu.*
▶ *order food when eating out.*
▶ *use numbers from 10 to 100.*
▶ *use the days of the week and months of the year.*
▶ *position words in sentences.*

CEFR: (A1) *Can handle numbers. Can indicate time by such phrases as last Friday and in November. Can get an idea of the content of simpler informational material (brochures) and short simple descriptions, especially if there is visual support.* **(A2)** *Can order a meal.*

Being polite

The informality of Danish culture extends to the language. Some people find the Danes surprisingly direct in their way of speaking, but nevertheless some level of politeness should be maintained. Danish does not have a word for *please*. Instead the Danes use **tak** (*thank you*) in many different situations. If you want to ask for something politely use **må jeg bede om** (*may I ask for*). A question can be answered with **ja, tak** (*yes, please*) or **nej, tak** (*no, thanks*).

> You will probably encounter many other uses of **tak**. More of them will be detailed in Unit 8.

 In Denmark you should always say **Tak for mad** after a meal. What do you think it means?

Vocabulary builder

03.01 Look at the words and fill in the missing translations. Then listen and try to imitate the pronunciation of the speakers.

FOOD AND DRINK

smørrebrød	*open sandwiches*
en pølse (-r)	*sausage*
en kylling (-er)	*chicken*
rejer	*prawns*
en bøf (-fer)	_____
en ost (-e)	*cheese*
en frikadelle (-r)	*meatballs*
en kartoffel (kartofler)	*potato*
et hvidløg (-)	*garlic*
et jordbær (-)	*strawberry*
et hindbær (-)	*raspberry*
chokolade	_____
is	_____
sodavand	*fizzy drinks*
danskvand	*mineral water*
appelsinjuice	*orange juice*
æblejuice	_____
øl	*beer*
hvidvin	*white wine*
rødvin	_____

NEW EXPRESSIONS

Look at the words and expressions that are used in the following conversation. Note their meanings.

Må jeg bede om …	*May I ask for …*
Kan jeg få …	*Can I have …*
Jeg vil gerne have …	*I would like to have …*
Ellers andet?	*Anything else?*
en flaske (-r)	*bottle*
flødeskum	*whipped cream*
en frokost (-er)	*lunch*
billig	*cheap*
at drikke	*to drink*
at snakke	*to talk*
Søbogård	*brand of organic fruit juice*

Conversation 1

 03.02 *Katrine and Louise are in a café for lunch. The waiter comes over to take their order.*

1 What food are they ordering?

Tjener	Hvad kunne I tænke jer?
Katrine	Kan jeg få en kyllingesalat?
Tjener	Vil du have noget at drikke?
Katrine	Ja, en cola, tak – og måske en latte og et stykke chokoladekage til dessert.
Louise	Jeg vil gerne bede om frikadeller med kartoffelsalat og en flaske Søbogård med hindbær, og så vil jeg gerne have et stykke jordbærtærte til dessert.
Tjener	Vil du have flødeskum til tærten?
Louise	Ja, tak.
Tjener	Skal I have noget vand?
Louise	Ja, tak – det ville være fint.
Tjener	Ellers andet?
Katrine	Nej, tak – det var det hele.

2 Listen to the conversation again. Find two different ways to ask for something.

3 How do you say *that is all* **in Danish?**

4 Look at the last three questions asked by the waiter. How do you think questions are constructed when not using a question word (hvem, hvad, hvor, etc.)?

 # Language discovery

1 ASKING QUESTIONS

In Danish you can ask a question simply by letting the subject and the verb swap places in a sentence.

Du drikker kaffe is a statement (*you drink coffee*).

Drikker du kaffe? is a question (*do you drink coffee?*)

Notice that it is exactly the same form of the verb you are using in both examples, whereas in English you would need to insert *do, is, are* and so on to ask the question.

2 NUMBERS TO 100

03.03 Here are the numbers 10 to 100. Listen to the pronunciation and repeat.

10	**ti**	60	**tres**
20	**tyve**	70	**halvfjerds**
30	**tredive**	80	**firs**
40	**fyrre**	90	**halvfems**
50	**halvtreds**	100	**ethundrede**

Danish does not have the most obvious system for numbers. You will probably need to listen to and repeat the numbers several times.

When saying a number the unit comes before the tens with **og** (*and*) in between. Look at these examples.

21	**enogtyve**	62	**toogtres**
35	**femogtredive**	74	**fireoghalvfjerds**
49	**niogfyrre**	88	**otteogfirs**
56	**seksoghalvtreds**	97	**syvoghalvfems**

3 DAYS OF THE WEEK AND MONTHS OF THE YEAR IN DANISH

03.04 Listen to how we say the days of the week and months of the year in Danish.

mandag, tirsdag, onsdag, torsdag, fredag, lørdag, søndag

Which of the days of the week do you think are named after the Nordic gods Odin, Tyr, Thor and Frigg?

03.05 januar, februar, marts, april, maj, juni, juli, august, september, oktober, november, december

Note that the days and the months are not written with a capital letter!

Different prepositions are used with the days of the week depending on what you want to say.

På mandag indicates the future (*on the Monday coming/next Monday*).

Om mandagen indicates a habit/regular activity (*on all/most Mondays*).

I mandags indicates a specific time in the past (*on last Monday*).

> Danes often refer to the number of the week rather than the dates, for example, **Vi holder ferie i uge 27 og 28** (*We are going on holiday week 27 and 28*), **Jeg kommer til Danmark i uge 48** (*I am coming to Denmark in week 48*).

4 WORD ORDER IN A SENTENCE

In the sentence **Louise drikker kaffe**, **Louise** is the subject and **drikker** is the verb.

If we want to specify that Louise is drinking coffee in a café we can add **på cafeen** either at the end of the sentence, **Louise drikker kaffe på cafeen**, or the beginning of the sentence, **På cafeen drikker Louise kaffe**.

Notice the verb and the subject in these two sentences.

Look at the following sentence: **Det var hyggeligt at spise frokost med dig Louise**.

In this sentence **det** is the subject and **var** is the verb so the subject comes before the verb.

If you say **Nej, søndag skal jeg arbejde**, **skal** is the verb and **jeg** is the subject, so the verb comes before the subject.

In English the subject always comes before the verb, unless it is a question. That is not the case in Danish. Unlike English, the verb quite often comes before the subject in a Danish sentence, even when it is not a question. The best rule to try and remember is that if the subject is not the first word in the sentence, then generally the verb comes first.

 Practice

1 **Turn these statements into questions. The first one has been done for you.**
   a Du elsker kaffe.   *Elsker du kaffe?*
   b Jens sover.
   c Hanne spiser frikadeller.
   d Jeg har 2 sønner.
   e De drikker vin.

2 **Write these numbers as figures.**
   a fireoghalvtreds
   b enogfirs
   c treogfyrre
   d seksogtredive
   e Nioghalvfems

3 Can you give the answers to these questions in Danish?
   a What day is it today?
   b Which month were you born?
   c Which day of the week is your birthday this year?
   d How would you say *see you on Thursday*?

4 Complete these two sentences.
   a Katrine spiser frokost med Louise _____
      (on Wednesdays)
   b Jeg var på cafe _____ (last Sunday)

5 Rewrite the sentences with the specified word at the start.
   a Louise arbejder søndag.
      Søndag _____
   b Katrine og Louise spiser frokost på en cafe
      På en cafe _____
   c Tjeneren kommer nu
      Nu _____

Conversation 2

03.06 **Katrine and Louise have finished their meal. Listen to the conversation.**

1 When are they going to meet again?

Katrine	Må vi bede om regningen?
Tjener	Ja, lige et øjeblik.
Katrine	Det var hyggeligt at spise frokost med dig Louise
Louise	Ja, det må vi gøre igen. Hvad med på lørdag?
Katrine	Nej, det kan jeg desværre ikke, men måske søndag?
Louise	Nej, søndag skal jeg arbejde. Så må vi prøve i næste uge. Jeg kan tirsdag eller onsdag.
Katrine	Onsdag kan jeg også.
Louise	Så siger vi det. Næste onsdag spiser vi frokost sammen igen.
Tjener	Her er regningen.
Katrine	356 kroner, det var billigt.
Louise	Så kommer vi her igen på onsdag!

2 Can you find three examples of the verb appearing before the
   subject in a sentence?

3 What is the Danish word for *the bill*?

4 Which days of the week are mentioned in the text?

> When eating out you are not obliged to leave a tip, service is normally included in your
> bill. However if a waiter has done a good job they always like to be appreciated with a
> bit extra.

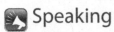 ## Speaking

Play the part of Sofie in this conversation.

Tjener	Hvad vil du gerne have?
Sofie	*(Can I have a sandwich with chicken and a coffee?)*
Tjener	Vil du have dessert?
Sofie	*(I would like chocolate cake.)*
Tjener:	Ellers andet
Sofie	*(No thanks, that is all.)*

 ## Reading

**Read the menu then try the speaking activity above again, but
order a starter, a main course and a dessert from the menu.**

Menu

Forretter
Rejecocktail
Hvidløgsbrød
Aspargessuppe

Hovedretter
Frokostbøf
Frikadellermed kartoffelsalat
Pizza med tomat og ost
Burger med Pommes fritter
Kyllinge filet med salat
Salat med laks

Desserter
Soft ice
Chokolademousse
Pandekager med is

Drikkevarer
Sodavand (cola, appelsin, sprite)
Danskvand
Øl
Hvidvin
Rødvin
Æblejuice

Test yourself

1 Write out these numbers as words.
  a 37
  b 81
  c 59
  d 26
  e 44

2 How would you order meatballs, potato salad and a beer?

3 How would you ask for the bill?

4 What is the Danish for these days of the week?
  a Sunday
  b Tuesday
  c Wednesday
  d Saturday

5 Put the words in the right order to make a sentence starting with the word indicated.
  a arbejder/mandag/i Århus/Katrine
     Mandag _____
  b spiser/chokoladekage/Louise/På cafeen
     På cafeen _____
  c Står/på bordet/vand/der
     På bordet _____

SELF CHECK

	I CAN ...
○	... read a menu.
○	... order food when eating out.
○	... use numbers from 10 to 100.
○	... use the days of the week and months of the year.
○	... position words in sentences.

Review 1

1 Read the following text and answer the questions.

Lene er gift med Jesper. De bor på Lolland Falster og de har tre børn, Sille, Amalie og Lukas. Hver fredag besøger børnene deres mormor, Lise som bor i Vordingborg. Jesper arbejder også i Vordingborg, han er arkitekt. Lene har en bror som er gift med Julie fra Frankrig, og de bor i Paris De har 2 drenge, som taler dansk og fransk. Lene kan også tale fransk, hun er lærer og underviser i fransk og engelsk. Hver sommer holder de ferie sammen i Frankrig og børnene kan lege med deres franske fætre.

- **a** What is Lise's relationship with Jesper?
- **b** What jobs do Lene and Jesper have?
- **c** How many grandchildren does Lise have?
- **d** How are Sille and Amalie related to the French boys?

 2 03.07 **Listen to the numbers and write them down.**

3 How do you say the following in Danish?

- **a** A man
- **b** The teacher
- **c** Doctors
- **d** The child
- **e** The children
- **f** A wife
- **g** Houses
- **h** The chickens

4 Put the names of the days of the week in the right order:

tirsdag, lørdag, onsdag, mandag, fredag, søndag, torsdag

5 03.08 **Jesper and Thomas bump into each other at the train station. Listen to their conversation and answer the questions.**

Thomas	Hej Jesper.
Jesper	Dav, hvordan går det?
Thomas	Det går fint, tak. Hvad med dig?
Jesper	Jo tak, jeg har det godt. Hvor skal du hen?
Thomas	Jeg skal til Svendborg og besøge min fætter. Han har åbnet en restaurant.

Jesper	Laver han maden selv?
Thomas	Ja, det gør han sammen med sin kone. Hvor skal du hen?
Jesper	Jeg skal på arbejde i Nyborg.
Thomas	Nu kommer mit tog. Vi ses på lørdag.
Jesper	Hej, hej.

  a Why is Thomas travelling?
  b Who has opened a restaurant?
  c Where is Jesper going?
  d How can you tell they are friends?

6 Underline the correct sentence in each of the following.

  a Jesper er arkitekt./Jesper er en arkitekt.
  b Pige hedder Mette./Pigen hedder Mette.
  c Han møder hun./Han møder hende.
  d Hver mandag går de på café./Hver mandag de går på café.

7 What would you say in the following situations?

  a How would you greet a friend?
  b What would you say if meeting somebody at 11am?
  c What would you say when leaving a business meeting?
  d What would you say when going to bed?
  e How would you ask for a coffee?
  f How would you ask for the bill?

På indkøb

Going shopping

In this unit you will learn how to:
▶ *go shopping.*
▶ *use adjectives such as colours.*
▶ *use modal verbs.*
▶ *talk about the weather.*

CEFR: (A1) *Can understand and use familiar everyday expressions and very basic phrases. Can ask people for things and give people things.* **(A2)** *Can write short, simple notes and messages relating to matters in areas of immediate needs.*

Money

The **penge** (*money*) used in Denmark is **kroner** and **øre**. Notes come in the values of 50kr, 100kr, 200kr, 500kr and 1000kr; coins come in 50 øre, 1kr, 2kr, 5kr, 10kr and 20kr. A price can still be shown as 45,95kr, even though you cannot physically pay 95 øre. If you are paying with **kontanter** (*cash*) the total amount will be rounded up or down to the nearest 50 øre.

Almost all Danes have a **Dankort**. Dankort is a national debit card that can be used in most places in Denmark. The vast majority of shops and restaurants in Denmark will accept foreign debit and credit cards, but some retailers in areas with fewer tourists might only accept Dankort.

Pengeautomat and **hæveautomat** are two words for the same thing. What do you think they are?

Vocabulary builder

04.01 **Look at the words and fill in the missing translations. Then listen and try to imitate the pronunciation of the Danish speakers.**

COLOURS

gul	*yellow*
rød	_____
grøn	_____
lilla	*purple*
blå	_____
sort	*black*
hvid	*white*
orange	_____
lyserød	*pink*
brun	*brown*

CLOTHING

tøj (-et)	*clothes*
bukser	*trousers*
en skjorte (-r)	*a shirt*
et slips (-)	*a tie*
en kjole (-r)	*a dress*
en nederdel (-e)	*a skirt*
en trøje (-r)	*a sweater*
sko	*shoes*
støvler	*boots*
et tørklæde (-r)	*scarf*
en jakke (-r)	_____

WEATHER

solskin	*sunshine*
regn	_____
blæst	*wind*
sne	_____
slud	*sleet*

NEW EXPRESSIONS

Look at the words and expressions that are used in the following conversation. Note their meanings.

at prøve	*to try*
en størrelse (-r)	*size*
ingen	*nobody* or *none*
en ekspedient(-er)	*shop assistant*
synes om	*think about (opinion)*
i stedet for	*instead*

Conversation 1

 04.02 *Lise and Lotte are out shopping.*

1 What do they buy?

Lise	Jeg skal have en ny kjole til festen på lørdag. Jeg kunne godt tænke mig en rød en.
Lotte	Lad os kigge herinde, her er både kjoler og bukser. Jeg vil gerne finde et par sorte bukser.
Lise	Hvad synes du om den her, den er både rød og orange?
Lotte	Den er flot, så skal du bare have et par røde sko til.
Lise	Jeg prøver den.
...	
Lise	Jeg tror den er lidt for lille, jeg prøver lige en størrelse 40 i stedet for.
Lotte	Passer den bedre?
Lise	Ja, det er meget bedre. Den snupper jeg. Har du fundet noget? Ville du ikke have et grønt tørklæde til din nye jakke?
Lotte	Jo, men der er ingen grønne tørklæder- men her er et flot rødt tørklæde.
Lise	Det er bare rigtig flot – det skal du købe!
Lotte	Ja, det tror jeg gør.

2 Answer the following questions.

   a Why does Lise want to buy a dress?
   b Does the dress fit Lise?
   c What size of dress does Lise buy?
   d What colour of clothing does Lotte buy?

3 Find all the places the colour red is mentioned. What do you notice?

 # Language discovery

1 ADJECTIVES

Adjectives such as colours look different depending on the word they are describing. Adjectives can be in their basic form, have a **t** added or an **e**.

Look at these examples. Can you spot the pattern for when to use the different endings?

en gul trøje	**en grøn jakke**	**Kjolen er rød**
et gult tørklæde	**et grønt hus**	**Huset er rødt**
4 gule jakker	**10 grønne æbler**	**Skoene er røde**

If the adjective is describing a word that normally has **en** in front then the basic form is used.

If the adjective is describing a word that normally has **et** in front then the adjective has a **t** added at the end.

If the adjective is describing something in the plural then the adjective has an **e** added at the end.

The **e** form is also used if the adjective comes after a possessive pronoun (**min**, **din** and so on, to be covered in Unit 5), or if after a demonstrative pronoun (**den**, **det**, to be covered in Unit 8).

Here are a few more examples:

en høj mand	*a tall man*
et højt hus	*a tall house*
en glad pige	*a happy girl*
tre glade piger	*three happy girls*
et smukt træ	*a beautiful tree*
en stor hund	*a big dog*
fire unge mænd	*four young men*

If an adjective already ends in a **t** (for example, **sort**), then the basic form and the **t** form will be the same.

Some adjectives will take a double consonant in the **e** form. For example, smuk becomes smukke in the **e** form.

Some adjectives are irregular and do not change as expected. A few of them are listed below. Can you spot the irregularities?

Basic form	't' form	'e' form
blå	blåt	blå
orange	orange	orange
grå	gråt	grå
lilla	lilla	lilla
lille (small)	lille	små (if for plural)
gammel	gammelt	gamle

2 SIZES

Here are some of the clothing sizes used in Denmark. The approximate conversion to UK and US sizes are in brackets, although it obviously varies between brands.

Women's dress sizes: 34 (8/4), 36 (10/6), 38 (12/8), 40 (14/10), 42 (16/12), 44 (18/14), 46 (20/16)

Men's waist sizes: 84/88 (32), 88/92 (33), 92/96 (34), 96/100 (36), 100/104 (38), 104/108 (40)

Men's collar sizes: 36 (14), 37 (14½), 38 (15), 39 (15½), 40 (15¾), 41 (16¼), 42 (16½), 43 (17)

3 MODAL VERBS

A modal verb is a verb that cannot be used on its own. It is normally followed by another verb in the infinitive. In English these are verbs such as: *can, will, must, may, shall*.

These are the most common Danish modal verbs.

Infinitive	Present tense	Meaning
at kunne	kan	A possibility: **Jeg kan komme til festen på lørdag** (*I can come to the party on Saturday*); **Kan jeg få en kop kaffe?** (*Can I have a cup of coffee please?*)
		Something learned: **Jeg kan tale dansk** (*I can speak Danish*)
		An ability: **Jeg kan ikke sove** (*I can't sleep*)
at måtte	må	Permission: **Du må gerne komme til festen på lørdag** (*You are welcome to come to the party on Saturday*)
		Necessity: **Jeg må ringe til lægen** (*I have to phone the doctor*)
at skulle	skal	Indicate future: **Jeg skal til fest på lørdag** (*I am going to a party on Saturday*)
		Command: **Du skal spise din broccoli nu!** (*You have to eat your broccoli now!*)
		Skal can be used without another verb to indicate that you are going somewhere: **Jeg skal hjem** (*I am going home*)

at ville	vil	A decision, expression of a will to do something: **Jeg vil til fest på lørdag** (*I want to go to a party on Saturday*)
		A desire, when combined with **gerne/godt**: **Jeg vil gerne til fest på lørdag** (*I would like to go to a party on Saturday*)
		Vil can be used without another verb to indicate where you want to go: **Jeg vil hjem** (*I want to go home*)
at burde	bør	Moral obligation: **Jeg bør tage til festen på lørdag** (*I ought to go to the party on Saturday*)

Here are some sentences from Conversation 1.

1 Jeg vil gerne finde et par sorte bukser

2 Det er bare rigtig flot – det skal du købe!

In Sentence 1 the modal verb is **vil**, the second verb is **finde** – which one of the options mentioned in the table above for the use of **vil** is used here?

In Sentence 2 the modal verb is **skal**, the second verb is **købe** – which one of the options mentioned in the table above for the use of **skal** is used here?

 Practice

1 Fill in the gaps in the table with the correct form of the adjective.

Basic form	't' form	'e' form
hvid	hvidt	hvide
ny		
		høje
	gammelt	
kold		
	stort	
		unge
smuk		
glad		

2 Fill in the correct form of the adjectives in these sentences.

   a Bordet er _____ (*black*)

   b Bukserne er _____ (*brown*)

   c Kjolen er _____ (*blue*)

   d Nederdelen er _____ (*pink*)

   e Skoene er _____ (*green*)

3 How would the following people ask for what they want in Danish?

   a A woman wearing a UK size 16 wants to buy a red dress.

   b A man wearing a UK/US collar size 15 wants to buy a blue shirt.

4 **Complete the sentences using a modal verb.**

   a _____ du tale dansk?
   b Børn _____ ikke drikke øl.
   c Jeg _____ gerne have en ny jakke.
   d Hvornår _____ du hjem?
   e _____ jeg bede om en sodavand?
   f Vi _____ drikke vand hver dag.

Conversation 2

 04.03 Lise and Lotte are finishing shopping, Listen to the conversation.

1 **What is the weather like?**

Lise	Vi må hellere komme videre inden det begynder at regne igen.
Lotte	Ja, lige nu skinner solen, så lad os gå ud. Vi skal bare lige betale.
Ekspedient	Et enkelt tørklæde – det bliver 256kr.
Lotte	Jeg betaler med Dankort.
Ekspedient	På beløbet?
Lotte	Kan jeg få den på firehundrede kroner, tak?
Ekspedient	Ja, værsgo, du får 144kr tilbage.
Lotte	Tak.
Lise	Lad os komme ud i solskinnet.

2 **What is the Danish word for** *sun*?

3 **What does Lotte buy?**

4 **How much is debited from Lotte's Dankort?**

> You will hear **På beløbet** quite often when paying by card. It literally means *on the amount*, and is asking if you want cashback. If you do want cashback you can either tell them the exact amount you want them to draw on your card, or you say the amount of cashback you want on top of the amount.

Reading

Read the text then answer the questions.

I Danmark skifter vejret ofte, så det er en god ide at se vejrudsigten. Om sommeren skinner solen, men der kan også være regn og lyn og torden. Når solen skinner er det dejligt vejr. Bornholm er det sted i Danmark hvor solen skinner mest. Om efteråret blæser det tit, specielt i Vestjylland. Når det regner og blæser er det dårligt vejr.Om vinteren er det koldt, og tit er der sne eller slud.

  a What is the word for *weather forecast*?
  b Which part of Denmark gets the most sunshine?
  c What kind of weather do you get in the autumn?
  d How would you say it *is lovely weather* in Danish?
  e How would you say *it is bad weather* in Danish?

Writing

You are going shopping on Strøget in Copenhagen in preparation for starting a new job. Write a list in Danish of the items you need to buy. Remember to include size and colour.

Speaking

04.04 Play the part of Karl in the conversation.

Hugo	Sikke det regner og blæser idag!
Karl	*(Yes, it is bad weather!)*
Hugo	Imorgen skal jeg på camping.
Karl	*(Tomorrow the sun will be shining.)*
Hugo	Hvordan ved du det?
Karl	*(From the weather forecast.)*

❓ Test yourself

1 Translate these sentences into Danish.
   a The shoes are black.
   b The house is red.
   c I have a blue scarf.
   d The children have five green apples.

2 Fill in the correct modal verb.
   a Jens _____ tale engelsk og dansk.
   b _____ jeg bede om en kop kaffe?
   c Jeg _____ til Danmark på mandag.
   d Jeg _____ gerne have en øl.

3 Describe what the weather is like today.

4 How would you do the following?
   a Ask for a white shirt
   b Ask for a skirt in a size 40
   c Ask if you can pay by card

SELF CHECK

I CAN ...

- ○ . . . go shopping.
- ○ . . . use adjectives such as colours.
- ○ . . . use modal verbs.
- ○ . . . talk about the weather.

5 Jeg vil gerne have en returbillet

Can I have a return ticket please?

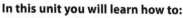

In this unit you will learn how to:
▶ *buy tickets for public transport.*
▶ *tell the time.*
▶ *use possessive pronouns in Danish.*

CEFR: (A1) *Can ask people for things and give people things.* **(A2)** *Can find specific, predictable information in simple everyday material such as advertisements, prospectuses, menus and timetables on familiar topics. Can get simple information about travel, use of public transport, give directions and buy tickets. Can describe plans, arrangements, habits and routines, past activities and personal experiences.*

Transport in Denmark

In Denmark public transport is generally quite good. You can travel by **tog** (*train*), **bus** or if in Copenhagen by **S-tog** (*subway*). Before boarding a train you have to get **en billet** (*ticket*) Tickets for trains can be booked online, or you can buy them at most stations at either a ticket office or from a machine. Children under the age of 12 usually travel for free on trains. Tickets for buses can be bought from the driver or quite often using an app on your phone. Many people have **et klippekort**, which is a multi-journey ticket that can be used in a combination of travel zones depending on how many **'klip'** you use and can be shared by two or more people. The newest option is **Rejsekort**. It is a travelcard with a chip, similar to a London Oystercard, which can be used on public transport all over Denmark.

When travelling by train people often buy **en pladsbillet** as an addition to their ticket. What do you think that is?

Vocabulary builder

05.01 Look at the words and phrases and complete the missing English expressions. Then listen and try to imitate the pronunciation of the speakers.

ON THE TRAIN

en banegård (-e)	*train station*
at skifte	*to change*
en billet (-ter)	*ticket*
en køreplan(-er)	_____
en stillekupe(-er)	*quiet compartment*
vinduesplads (-er)	_____
gangplads(-er)	*aisle seat*
ankomst	*arrival*
afgang	*departure*
en perron(-er)	*platform*
et spor (-)	*track*

NEW WORDS AND EXPRESSIONS

Jeg vil gerne have en billet til ...	*I would like a ticket to ...*
Hvor meget koster en billet til ...	*How much is a ticket to ...?*
Er det et direkte tog?	*Is that a direct train?*
Toget afgår fra spor 4	*The train leaves from platform 4*
en kuffert(-er)	*suitcase*
tung	*heavy*
en lomme (-r)	*pocket*

Conversation 1

05.02 Sanne and Simon want to travel from Roskilde to Hobro. They are at the train station buying tickets.

1 When are they travelling back?

Sanne	Jeg vil gerne have to returbilletter til Hobro.
Personale	Ja, skal I have pladsbilletter?
Sanne	Ja, tak – det må vi hellere.
Personale	Det næste tog til Hobro kører kl. 10.08, men så skal I skifte i Odense. Ellers kan I vente til 10.45, det tog kører direkte til Hobro.

---

5 Jeg vil gerne have en returbillet Can I have a return ticket please?   43

Sanne	Skal vi ikke vente til 10.45, mine tasker er så tunge?
Simon	Det kan vi sagtens, kvart i elleve lyder fint.
Personale	Og hvornår skal I hjem igen?
Simon	På søndag ved middagstid.
Personale	Der er et direkte tog fra Hobro til Roskilde kl. 12.21
Sanne	Det lyder fint.
Personale	Skal det være stillekupe?
Sanne	Nej, vi vil gerne snakke sammen på turen.
Personale	Det bliver 858 kr.
Personale	Værsgo – her er jeres billetter.
Sanne	Tak skal du have.
Simon	Skal jeg tage vores billetter i lommen, eller vil du hellere beholde din egen?
Sanne	Ja tag dem i lommen. Klokken er kun fem minutter over ti, så vi har masser af tid inden toget kører – skal vi gå i kiosken og købe nogle sodavand til rejsen?

2 Read the dialogue again and answer the questions.
   a Why do they travel on the 10.45 rather than the 10.05?
   b What do they want to do during the journey?
   c What time is it when they have finished buying tickets?

3 Find the Danish words for *my*, *your* **and** *our* **in the dialogue.**

4 When telling the time, how do you think you say *past* **and** *to* **in Danish?**

 ## Language discovery

1 POSSESSIVE PRONOUNS

Here are the possessive pronouns in Danish.

min/mit/mine	*my*	**dets**	*its*
din/dit/dine	*your* (singular)	**sin/sit/sine**	*his/her* (own)
hans	*his*	**vores**	*our*
hendes	*her*	**jeres**	*your* (plural)
dens	*its*	**deres**	*their*

If you look at the word for *my* and *your* you can see that there are three versions for each. Thinking about what you learned in Unit 4 about adjectives changing, what do you think the difference is between **min**, **mit** and **mine**?

Min and **din** changes depending on the word they are relating to. You use **min** or **din** if it is connected to a word that normally takes **en** in front, **mit** or **dit** if the word normally takes **et** in front and **mine** or **dine** if the word is plural.

Here are some examples.

min mand (*my husband*)   **mit barn** (*my child*)   **mine børn** (*my children*)
din kop (*your cup*)   **dit hus** (*your house*)   **dine huse** (*your houses*)

You will have noticed there are two words for *its*; it can either be **dens** or **dets**. Using your knowledge of Danish nouns what do you think the difference is?

Again it comes down to the difference between words that have **en** in front and those with **et**, but the important factor is what word *its* is replacing.

Han tog hundens legetøj (*He took the dog's toy*) becomes **Han tog dens legetøj** (*He took its toy*).

Han tog dyrets legetøj (*He took the animal's toy*) becomes **Han tog dets legetøj** (*He took its toy*).

You probably noticed in the list as well the words **sin/sit/sine**. These are possessive pronouns with no English equivalent. They are used when the object being talked about is 'owned' by the subject of the sentence. **Sin/sit/sine** would normally translate into English as *his*, *her* or *its*, but it is used specifically when you mean *his own*, *her own* or *its own*. Here is an example to show the difference.

Nikolaj elsker sin kone.   *Nikolaj loves his wife.* (This means Nikolaj loves his (own) wife.)

Nikolaj elsker hans kone.   *Nikolaj loves his wife.* (This indicates that Nikolaj loves someone who is a wife but not his own.)

Nikolaj is the subject of the sentence, so by using **sin** we show the direct relation to Nikolaj.

When using **hans** there is no direct relation to the subject, so it becomes somebody else's wife.

Here is another example.

Gitte tager sit halstørklæde på. *Gitte puts on her (own) scarf.*

Gitte tager hendes halstørklæde på. *Gitte puts on her scarf (indicating some other female's scarf).*

Obviously the difference between **sin/sit/sine** is the same as shown above for **min/mit/mine** or **din/dit/dine**, so we would say:

Nikolaj elsker sin kone. Nikolaj elsker sit hus.

Nikolaj elsker sine børn.

Please note that **sin/sit/sine** can never be at the beginning of a sentence and it cannot be the subject of the sentence!

> Don't worry too much about upsetting people by confusing **hans/hendes/sin**. Normally the context will show what you mean, and even some Danes get this one wrong occasionally.

2 TELLING THE TIME

The Danes use the 24-hour clock for timetables, TV schedules and similar situations where the information will be read rather than spoken. When speaking they tend to go by the 12-hour system, however, they never use a.m. or p.m. If they need to indicate whether it is 9 a.m. or 9 p.m., they would say **klokken ni om morgenen** or **klokken ni om aftenen**.

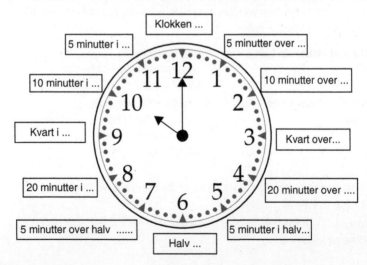

It is important to note that in Danish you are not indicating 'half past', but 'half way to'. So in Danish 2:30 would be **halv tre**, 4:30 would be **halv fem**. What would 9:30 be?

Twenty-five minutes past is usually described as five minutes to the half hour.

For example:

2:25	fem **minutter i halv tre**
6:25	fem **minutter i halv syv**

Twenty-five minutes to is described as five minutes past the half hour.

4:35	**fem minutter over halv fem**
12.35	**fem minutter over halv et**

Practice

1 Insert the correct possessive pronoun. The first one has been done for you

   a Gitte har en hund. Det er _hendes_ hund .
   b Jeg har 3 børn. Det er _____ børn.
   c Vi købte 2 togbilletter. Det er _____ billetter.
   d De har et stort hus. Det er _____ store hus.
   e Du har et tørklæde på. Det er _____ tørklæde.
   f I har ferie imorgen. Det er _____ ferie imorgen.
   g Dyret har mad. Det er _____ mad.
   h Peter har en kat. Det er _____ kat.

2 What goes in the gap? Choose from hans, hendes, sin, sit or sine.

   a Jens er glad for _____ arbejde.
   b Her er Søren. _____ kone hedder Lene.
   c Susanne mødte _____ veninder i teatret.
   d Lone elsker _____ mand.
   e Lone og _____ mand kommer til frokost.
   f Jeg skal i teatret med Jens og _____ kone.

3 What is the time on these clocks?

03:20   12:50   10:55

12:15   11:35   11:30

10:15   06:45   03:35

Conversation 2

05.03 *Søren is waiting at the bus stop when bus number 31 arrives.*

1 What is his destination and which bus can he get there?

Søren	Dav, kører du til Østergade?
Buschauffør	Nej det gør jeg ikke. Jeg kører til Nørreport.
Søren	Kan du fortælle mig hvilken bus der kører til Østergade?
Buschauffør	Du skal med en 14 herfra, eller en 26 stopper rundt om hjørnet.
Søren	Hvornår går den næste 14?
Buschauffør	Det ved jeg desværre ikke, men de går tit, så der kommer nok snart en.
Søren	Tak for hjælpen.
Buschauffør	Det var så lidt.

2 Answer these questions.

   a Where does bus number 26 leave from?

   b Is bus number 14 frequent?

Reading

Look at the bus timetable and answer the questions.

   a If you lived close to Nørregade but worked in Skolegade which bus would you get to be at work for 8 a.m. on a Monday?

Storegade – Banegården – Kirkegade

		Hverdage undt.lørdage ikke 24/12, 31/12 og 5/6											
regade	afg	06.05	07.05	S07.25	08.10	10.10	12.10	14.10	S15.10	16.10	18.10
regade		06.09	07.09	07.29	08.14	10.14	12.14	14.14	15.14	16.14	18.14
nsterparken		06.12	07.12	07.32	08.17	10.17	12.17	14.17	15.17	16.17	18.17
egården	ank	06.16	07.16	07.36	08.21	10.21	12.21	14.21	15.21	16.21	18.21
egården	afg	06.20	07.20	07.40	08.25	10.25	12.25	14.25	15.25	16.25	18.25
levej		06.24	07.24	07.44	08.29	10.29	12.29	14.29	15.29	16.29	18.29
legade		06. 30	06.30	07.50	08.35	10.35	12.35	14.35	15.35	16.35	18.35
egade	ank	06.35	07.35	07.55	08.40	10.40	12.40	14.40	15.40	16.40	18.40

Storegade – Banegården – Kirkegade

		Lørdage samt 31/12 og 5/6					Søndage samt 24/12			
Storegade	afg	07.05	09.05	12.10	16.10	**A**18.10	09.05	12.10	**B**16.10	**B**18.10
Nørregade		07.09	09.09	12.14	16.14	18.14	09.09	12.14	16.14	18.14
Blomsterparken		07.12	09.12	12.17	16.17	18.17	09.12	12.17	16.17	18.17
Banegården	ank	07.16	09.16	12.21	16.21	18.21	09.16	12.21	16.21	18.21
Banegørden	afg	07.20	09.20	12.25	16.25	18.25	09.20	12.25	16.25	18.25
Møllevej		07.24	09.24	12.29	16.29	18.29	09.24	12.29	16.29	18.29
Skolegade		06.30	09.30	12.35	16.35	18.35	09.30	12.35	16.35	18.35
Kirkegade	ank	07.35	09.35	12.40	16.40	18.40	09.35	12.40	16.40	18.40

S – Kører kun skoledage
A – Kører ikke 31/12
B - Kører ikke 24/12

b Would that be the same if it was a school holiday?

c If you wanted to catch a train at 4.30 p.m., which bus should you get?

> When saying the time using the 24 hr clock in Danish you just say the two numbers, for example 15.37 is pronounced 'femten syvogtredive'. If there was a 0 involved you would say 'nul', for example 12.04 is pronounced tolv nul fire. Note as well that when writing the 24 hr clock a full stop is used between the numbers rather than a colon.

Writing

Look at the timetable again. You are visiting a friend in Kirkegade. You are invited for dinner on Friday night. Write a short text message to your friend describing when and where you are getting on and off the bus.

> When saying the time using the 24 hr clock in Danish you just say the two numbers, for example 15.37 is pronounced 'femten syvogtredive'. If there was a 0 involved you would say 'nul', for example 12.04 is pronounced tolv nul fire. Note as well that when writing the 24 hr clock a full stop is used between the numbers rather than a colon.

Speaking

05.04 Play the part of Ida in the conversation.

Ida	*(I would like a return ticket to Nyborg.)*
Personale	Ja, tak – skal du have pladsbillet.
Ida	*(Yes please.)*
Personale	Hvornår vil du rejse.
Ida	*(11.45.)*
Personale	Og hvornår skal du hjem.
Ida	*(Tomorrow at 13.05.)*
Personale	Det bliver 238kr. Værsgo her er din billet.
Ida	*(Thank you.)*

? Test yourself

1 Insert the correct possessive pronoun.

   a Jeg har et glas. Det er _____ glas.

   b Asger cykler hver dag. Det er _____ cykel.

   c Har du _____ hund med?

   d Her bor vi. Det er _____ hus.

   e Susan elsker _____ børn.

   f Alle børnene havde _____ jakker på.

2 How would you say these times in Danish?

   a 2:15

   b 20:00

   c 5:30

   d 16:10

   e 10:25

3 How would you do the following?

   a Ask for a return ticket for the train for Roskilde

   b Ask for a seat reservation in the quiet compartment

   c Ask for the platform number for the train for Nyborg

6 Hvor ligger Rådhuspladsen?

Where is the town square?

In this unit you will learn how to:
▶ *ask and give directions.*
▶ *use the imperative form of verbs.*
▶ *use ordinal numbers.*

CEFR: (A1) *Can fill in forms of personal details (name, address, registration) of self or others.* **(A2)** *Can ask for and give directions. Can understand everyday signs and notices: in public places, such as streets, restaurants, railway stations, and work places such as instructions, directions, warnings. Can make arrangements to meet, decide where to go and what to do.*

📷 Compound words

Danish has a lot of rather long words, because compound words are very common. For example, in English *train station* is still two words, but in Danish *tog* and *station* join together to become *togstation*. So if you have two, three or even more words joining together the result can be rather long, like **busstoppested**. Many street names are just one word, with **vej** (*road*) or **gade** (*street*) added to the main word, for example, **Nørregade** (*North Street*) or **Møllevej** (*Mill Road*). Here are a few more examples of compound words: **et trafiklys** (*traffic light*), **et vejskilt** (*road sign*), **en trafikprop** (*traffic jam*), **en cykelsti** (*cycle path*), **en cykelhjelm** (*bike helmet*), **vejarbejde** (*roadworks*). The longest word used officially in Denmark had 51 letters!

How many words have been compounded in **cykelhjelmskampagne** and what does it mean?

> It is always the last part of the compound word that determines whether it should have **en** or **et** in front.

Vocabulary builder

06.01 Look at the words and phrases and complete the missing English expressions. Then listen and try to imitate the pronunciation of the speakers.

GIVING DIRECTIONS

højre	*right*
venstre	*left*
ligeud	*straight ahead*
at dreje	*turn*
en frakørsel (-er)	*exit*
en rundkørsel (-er)	_____
et kryds (-)	*junction*
derovre	*over there*
ved	*by*
efter	_____
før	*before*

NEW WORDS AND EXPRESSIONS

Undskyld	*Excuse me/Sorry*
Kan du fortælle mig …?	*Can you tell me …?*
Anden vej til højre	*Second road to the right*

Conversation 1

06.02 *Magnus has just arrived in the airport and needs to get to his hotel in Esbjerg. He goes to the information desk to ask how to get there.*

1 What does the person at the information desk suggest?

Magnus	Undskyld, hvordan kommer jeg nemmest til Esbjerg herfra?
Information	Du kan tage bussen til Esbjerg. Gå ud ad døren derovre og så til højre, der holder busserne. Tag så bus nummer 44, den kører til Esbjerg.
Magnus	Bus nummer 44, tak!

In Esbjerg Magnus asks Kasper at the bus terminal how to get to his hotel in Jyllandsgade.

2 Is the hotel far away?

Magnus	Undskyld, kan du fortælle mig hvor Jyllandsgade og Hotel Danica er?
Kasper	Ja, du skal ligeud hen ad Jernbanegade, og så drej til venstre i det første kryds hen ad Nygårdsgade. Bliv ved med at gå lige ud og efter det femte kryds lige efter Skt Nikolaj Kirken drej til højre. Det er Jyllandsgade, og der er hotel Danica.
Magnus	Ok, drej til venstre i det første kryds og så til højre i det femte kryds. Hvor lang tid tror du det tager?
Kasper	10–15 minutter at gå tror jeg. Ellers kan du finde en taxa nede ved togstationen.
Magnus	Jeg tror, jeg går. Det er ikke så langt. Tak for hjælpen.

3 Find all the sentences where somebody tells Magnus where to go. Look at the verbs and see if you can find a pattern?

4 What is the Danish word for *fifth*?

5 How would you say *down by the train station* **in Danish?**

 # Language discovery

1 IMPERATIVE FORM OF VERBS

The imperative form of the verb is what is used when giving an order or directions. For example, **drej til højre** (*turn right*), **gå ud** (*get out*). As you know from Unit 1, most verbs in Danish end in **-e** in the infinitive (**at dreje**, for example), so to make that into a command you simply remove the **e** (**drej!**)

At køre becomes **kør!** (drive!)

At finde becomes **find!** (find!)

If the verb has a double consonant before the **e**, then one of the consonants disappears as well.

At sidde beomes **sid!** (sit!)

At drikke becomes **drik!** (drink!)

A verb that ends in one of the other vowels will normally remain unchanged in the imperative form.

At gå becomes **gå!** (go!)

At bo becomes **bo!** (live!)

2 ADVERBS OF PLACE

Adverbs of place tell us where something happens. In English that could be, for example, *up*, *down*, *near* or *out*. In Conversation 1 we saw the sentence **Ellers kan du finde en taxa nede ved togstationen**. **Nede** (*down*) is an adverb of place. ·

We could change the sentence slightly to **Gå ned til togstationen og find en taxa**. What happens to the word **nede**?

In Danish adverbs of place have two forms depending on whether there is movement or not. If there is no movement happening the adverb of place will end in 'e'.

The main adverbs of place in Danish are:

ud/ude (out)   ned/nede (down) ·

ind/inde (in)   hjem/hjemme (home) ·

op/oppe (up)   hen/henne (no English equivalent)

Jeg går ud.	I am going out.
Jeg er ude.	I am out.
Manden går op på loftet.	The man is going up to the loft.
Manden er oppe på loftet.	The man is up in the loft.
Drengen løber hen til sin mor.	The boy runs to his mother.
Drengen er henne hos sin mor.	The boy is by his mother.

3 ORDINAL NUMBERS

Here are the ordinal numbers in Danish up to 31st.

1st	**første**	*12th*	**tolvte**	*23rd*	**treogtyvende**
2nd	**anden**	*13th*	**trettende**	*24th*	**fireogtyvende**
3rd	**tredje**	*14th*	**fjortende**	*25th*	**femogtyvende**
4th	**fjerde**	*15th*	**femtende**	*26th*	**seksogtyvende**
5th	**femte**	*16th*	**sekstende**	*27th*	**syvogtyvende**
6th	**sjette**	*17th*	**syttende**	*28th*	**otteogtyvende**
7th	**syvende**	*18th*	**attende**	*29th*	**niogtyvende**
8th	**ottende**	*19th*	**nittende**	*30th*	**tredivte**
9th	**niende**	*20th*	**tyvende**	*31st*	**enogtredivte**
10th	**tiende**	*21st*	**enogtyvende**		
11th	**elvte**	*22nd*	**toogtyvende**		

From 40 to 49 adding **-tyvende** at the end will make the number ordinal (for example, **toogfyrretyvende** is *42nd*).

From 50 onwards all numbers become ordinal numbers by adding **-indstyvende** to the number (for example, **halvfjerdsindtyvende** is *70th*).

However, ordinal numbers are primarily used for dates, floors in buildings and school classes, so you are unlikely to ever need them above 31st.

> When talking about birthdays Danish does not use ordinal numbers like we do in English. So a *30th birthday* is simply **30-års fødselsdag**, *50th birthday* is **50-års fødselsdag**.

To write ordinal numbers as figures, simply add a full stop after the number.

1. **første**

2. **anden**

18. **attende**

Dates can be written in different ways, but most common are **27. september 2014** and **27.09.14**.

Practice

1 **Put these verbs in the imperative form.**
   a At dreje
   b At købe
   c At snakke
   d At gå
   e At spise
   f At køre

2 **Circle the correct adverb from the two options given.**
   a Lise bor op/oppe på 4. etage.
   b Vi går ud/ude og spiser.
   c Johan er ind/inde i huset.
   d Er du hjem/hjemme?

3 Write the ordinal number in words.

  a Astrid går i (3.) _____ klasse.

  b Jeg bor på (5.) _____ etage.

  c Toke har fødselsdag den (21.) _____ januar.

  d Oskar går i (7.) _____ klasse.

  e Ditte har fødselsdag den (14.) _____ april.

4 Write these dates in a number format. The first one has been done for you.

  a Syvogtyvende september = *21.9*

  b Enogtredivte juli

  c Sekstende april

  d Sjette januar

  e Elvte november

  f Niogtyvende marts

Reading

1 Match the English description of these road signs to the Danish description.

  a Rundkørsel
  b Parkering forbudt
  c Børn på/ved vejen
  d Risiko for kødannelse
  e Bump på vejen
  f Standsning forbudt
  g Delt sti, gående til venstre, cyklister til højre
  h Risiko for glat vej
  i Ensrettet
  j Farlig rabat
  k Tættere bebygget område
  l Ubetinget vigepligt

  1 Risk of queues
  2 Roundabout
  3 Children on/near the road
  4 Dangerous verge
  5 No parking
  6 Speed bumps on road
  7 Duty to give way to approaching traffic
  8 No stopping
  9 One way
  10 Built-up area
  11 Risk of icy road
  12 Shared path, pedestrians left, bicycles right

2 Now match the descriptions to the pictures.

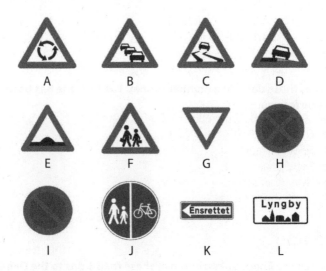

Conversation 2

 06.03 *Magnus arrives at the hotel and goes to the reception desk.*

1 How long is he staying for?

Magnus	Dav, jeg har bestilt et værelse.
Receptionisten	Ja, hvad er navnet.
Magnus	Magnus Johansen.
Receptionisten	Ja, 3 nætter med ankomst den 23. juli og afrejse den 26. juli.
Magnus	Ja, det er korrekt.
Receptionisten	Hvis du udfylder formen her, så finder jeg nøglen.
Magnus	Værsgo.
Receptionisten	Her er nøglen. Det er værelse 35, det er oppe på tredje etage. Gå igennem den grønne dør, til højre er trapperne og til venstre er elevatoren.
Magnus	Tak, jeg tager elevatoren op.

2 Which floor is Magnus's room on?

3 How does he get there?

Writing

Fill in this hotel registration form with your own details.

Fornavn _____

Efternavn _____

Adresse _____

Tlf. _____

Mobil _____

Nationalitet _____

Dato for ankomst _____

Dato for afrejse _____

Antal gæster _____

Morgenmad ja ☐ nej ☐ (sæt kryds)

Speaking

06.04 **Jakob and Sten are talking about when to meet again. Play the part of Sten.**

Jakob	Hvornår skal vi mødes igen? Jeg kan d. 23. april.
Sten	*(I can do the 23rd or the 25th April.)*
Jakob	Lad os sige d.23. så. Hvor skal vi mødes?
Sten	*(By Hotel Danica. We can eat lunch there.)*
Jakob	Det lyder fint. Hvilket tidspunkt?
Sten	*(12.30.)*
Jakob	Det siger vi.
Sten	*(See you on the 23rd.)*

Test yourself

1 How would you ask for assistance in the following circumstances?
   a Finding Hotel Scandinavia
   b Getting from the airport to Valby
   c Finding the restaurant in a hotel

2 Complete these sentences by translating the word in brackets and write it in the imperative form.
   a _____ til højre i krydset (to turn)
   b _____ ligeud (to drive)
   c _____ til venstre i det tredje kryds (walk)

3 Score out the incorrect adverb from the two options given.
   a Hvor skal du hen/henne?
   b Jeg går op/oppe til Hanne
   c Bussen holder ned/nede ved stationen
   d Kom ind/inde!

4 How would you write the date of your birthday in Danish?

5 How would you say that date in Danish?

1 Insert the adjective in the correct form.

a Jette har tre _____ æbler. (*green*)

b Træet er meget _____ . (*tall*)

c Lotte er _____ fordi hun har _____ sko på. (*happy/new*)

d Astrid har en _____ jakke og et _____ tørklæde. (*black/yellow*)

e Jens' bil er meget _____ . (*old*)

2 06.05 Listen to the times and write them down using digital format.

3 Insert a modal verb to complete the sentences.

a Simon's bil _____ køre hurtigt.

b _____ jeg bede om en øl.

c Jeg _____ gerne have en ny bil.

d Du _____ spise dine tomater!

4 Read the weather forecast and answer the questions.

Vejrudsigten for imorgen er igen regn og blæst det meste af dagen med temperaturer omkring 7 grader. Det er typisk efterårsvejr. På Sjælland kommer solen muligvis frem, men Nordjylland kan forvente regn hele dagen.

a What weather is expected the next day?

b What season is it?

c Where might the sun show?

5 Translate these sentences into Danish, make sure to use the correct possessive pronoun.

a I have your tickets in my pocket.

b Our children are called Peter and Louise.

c There is Sophie, it is her dress.

d He loves his wife.

e It is their house.

6 06.06 **Asger is asking Nikolaj for directions to the train station. Listen to the conversation and answer the questions.**

Asger	Kan du fortælle mig, hvordan jeg finder togstationen?
Nikolaj	Ja, det er nemt nok. Kør ligeud indtil du kommer til. Vestergade. Drej til venstre i krydset. Når du kommer til rundkørslen skal du tage den tredje frakørsel, så ligger togstationen til højre.
Asger	OK fint, ligeud, så til venstre, tredje frakørsel i rundkørslen og så ligger stationen til højre.
Nikolaj	Ja, lige præcis.
Asger	Tak, det prøver jeg.

   a Where should he go at the junction?
   b Which exit should he take from the roundabout?
   c Is the station to the left or the right?

7 Turn these sentences into orders using the imperative form of the verbs.
   a Du drejer til venstre i krydset.
   b Du bør drikke vand hver dag.
   c Du skal sætte dig på stolen.
   d Du skal skrive dit navn her.

8 Write these ordinal numbers as figures.
   a enogtyvende
   b trettende
   c ottende
   d enogtredivte
   e fjortende
   f fjerde

7 *Hvad lavede du igår?*

What did you do yesterday?

In this unit you will learn to:
▶ *use verbs in different past tenses.*
▶ *express likes and dislikes.*

CEFR: (A2) *Can explain what he likes or dislikes. Can catch the main point in short, clear, simple messages and announcements. Can write short, simple imaginary biographies and simple poems about people.*

Politics

Politics in Denmark can seem complicated. **Folketinget** (*Parliament*) has 179 **medlemmer**, four of which are elected in **Grønland** and **Færøerne** (*Faroe Islands*). **Folketinget** is based at **Christiansborg**. There is a multitude of **partier** (*parties*) in Denmark and the differences between some of the parties can appear very subtle to an outsider. **Regeringen** (*the government*) is always a coalition of some kind led by **Statsministeren** (*the Prime Minister*), and quite regularly also **en mindretalsregering** (*minority government*). **Valg** (*elections*) have to happen at least every four years and **folketingsmedlemmer** are elected in a system of proportional representation. A party has to get a minimum of 2 per cent of the overall vote to get any **pladser** (*seats*).

 Where do you think the political TV drama *Borgen* got its name from?

Vocabulary builder

07.01 **Look at the words and phrases and complete the missing English expressions. Then listen and try to imitate the pronunciation of the speakers.**

AT SCHOOL

kedeligt	*boring*
en historie (-r)	*a story*
et frikvarter(-)	*break time (at school)*
billedkunst	*art (subject at school)*
idræt	*physical education*
matematik	_____
historie	_____
fysik/kemi	_____
madkundskab	*home economics*
natur/teknologi	_____
at regne	*to do sums*
at gange	*to multiply*
at male	*to paint*
en time	*lesson*
at skrive	*to write*

NEW WORDS AND EXPRESSIONS

allerede	*already*
igår	*yesterday*
i sidste uge	*last week*
i sidste måned	*last month*
Sidste år	*last year*
at have travlt	*to be busy*
en gang imellem	*once in a while*
bagefter	*afterwards*

Conversation 1

07.02 *Sanne is asking her daughter Frederikke what she did in school.*

1 How many different subjects did she do?

Sanne	Hvad har du lavet i skolen idag?
Frederikke	I første time havde vi dansk. Det var lidt kedeligt for vi sad bare og læste hele tiden. Jeg vil hellere skrive historier.
Sanne	Ja, men det har I jo gjort mange gange, man skal også læse en gang imellem.
Frederikke	Men jeg har læst så mange bøger allerede. Det var sjovere at have idræt. Vi spillede håndbold. Før spisefrikvarteret havde vi engelsk. Jeg kan rigtig godt lide Mette.
Sanne	Ja, Mette er en fin lærer.
Frederikke	Efter spisefrikvarteret havde vi matematik. Vi regnede og snakkede om at gange og dividere. Heldigvis havde vi billedkunst bagefter, hvor vi malede et stort billede. Det var sjovt.
Sanne	Det lyder som en god dag.

2 Find all uses of the verb *to read.* **How many different versions of the verb are there?**

3 How would you say *I like ...* **in Danish?**

4 Find an expression in the dialogue that indicates a preference for something else.

> In Danish schools children normally call the teacher by their first name. The school day is structured into specialized lessons with different teachers even from the first year of school.

 # Language discovery

1 PAST TENSES

In Danish verbs have three tenses for describing something in the past:

▶ **Datid** (*past*); **snakkede** = *talked*
▶ **Førnutid** (*past perfect*); **har snakket** = *have talked*
▶ **Førdatid** (*pluperfect*); **havde snakket** = *had talked*

This is the same pattern as in English.

Datid is used for something that has been completed and/or happened at a specified time in the past, for example:

Jeg spiste smørrebrød til frokost.

Jeg boede i London fra 2003 til 2007.

Datid can be constructed in three different ways.

1 Add -(e)de to the infinitive, for example:

At arbejde becomes **arbejdede** (*to work* becomes *worked*)

At cykle becomes **cyklede** (*to cycle* becomes *cycled*)

At bo becomes **boede** (*to live* becomes *lived*)

2 Add -te to the very basic form of the verb (the infinitive without the e at the end), for example:

At spise becomes **spiste** (*to eat* becomes *ate*)

At læse becomes **læste** (*to read* becomes *read*)

At købe becomes **købte** (*to buy* becomes *bought*)

3 There are also verbs that are formed irregularly in this tense, for example:

At have becomes **havde** (*to have* becomes *had*)

At sige becomes **sagde** (*to say* becomes *said*)

At gå becomes **gik** (*to go* becomes *went*)

At være becomes **var** (*to be* becomes *was*)

Unfortunately there is no specific rule to let you know if a verb belongs to Group 1, 2 or 3, but some dictionaries will tell you (especially the official Danish spelling dictionary, **Retskrivningsordbogen**). The glossary at the back of this book also includes information on past tenses for all verbs listed and at the end of this unit there is a list of some of the irregular verbs.

Førnutid is used for things that still remain the same and/or where the time is not relevant, for example:

Jeg har spist smørrebrød til frokost i mere end 14 år. (I have eaten open sandwiches for lunch for more than 14 years)

Jeg har boet i London. (I have lived in London)

Førnutid consists of the past participle of the verb + **har** or occasionally **er**.

The past participle ends in **t**, so for the three groups of verbs it looks like this:

1 The -de gets replaced by t, for example:

At arbejde becomes **arbejdede** and then **har abejdet** (*to work/worked/have worked*)

At cykle becomes **cyklede** and then **har cyklet** (*to cycle/cycled/have cycled*)

At bo becomes **boede** and then **har boet** (*to live/lived/have lived*)

2 The e is taken away from the -te, for example:

At spise becomes **spiste** and then **har spist** (*to eat/ate/have eaten*)

At læse becomes **læste** and then **har læst** (*to read/read/have read*)

At købe becomes **købte** and then **har købt** (*to buy/bought/have bought*)

3 The irregular verbs stay irregular, but they do end in t, for example:

At have becomes **havde** and then **har haft** (*to have/had/have had*)

At sige becomes **sagde** and then **har sagt** (*to say/said/have said*)

At gå becomes **gik** and then **har/er gået** (*to go/went/have gone or are gone*)

Only verbs that indicate movement can have **er** rather than **har**, for example: **er gået**, **er løbet**, **er blevet**.

Førdatid is constructed in the same way as **førnutid**, except that rather than using **har/er** in front you use **havde/var**, for example:

Han havde haft travlt.   *He had been busy.*

Vi havde købt 2 øl.   *We had bought two beers.*

07.03 2 PREFERENCES

There are different ways to express your preferences in Danish.

If you are just indicating something you like you can use **Jeg kan godt lide**, for example:

Jeg kan godt lide at spille fodbold. *I like playing football.*

Jeg kan godt lide danske film.   *I like Danish films.*

If you are saying that you love something use **Jeg elsker**, for example:

Jeg elsker smørrebrød.   *I love smørrebrød.*

For something you don't like you can use **Jeg kan ikke lide**, for example:

Jeg kan ikke lide at køre i bus.　　*I don't like going by bus.*

Jeg kan ikke lide tomater.　　*I don't like tomatoes.*

If you want to be more polite you can say **Jeg bryder mig ikke om**, for example:

Jeg bryder mig ikke om tomater.　　*I am not keen on tomatoes.*

If you want to indicate a preference of one thing over another you can choose from the following phrases.

Jeg kan bedre lide ... end ...

Jeg kan bedre lide jazz end pop.　　*I like jazz music better than pop music.*

Jeg vil hellere ... end ...

Jeg vil hellere cykle end køre i bil.　　*I would rather cycle than drive.*

Jeg foretrækker ... fremfor ...

Jeg foretrækker at cykle fremfor at gå.　　*I prefer cycling to walking.*

3 IRREGULAR VERBS

This table shows some of the irregular verbs in Danish in the present, past and past perfect tenses.

INFINITIVE	PRESENT	PAST	PAST PERFECT
at blive *(to become)*	bliver	blev	er blevet
at burde *(modal verb)*	bør	burde	har burdet
at bære *(to carry)*	bærer	bar	har båret
at drikke *(to drink)*	drikker	drak	har drukket
at finde *(to find)*	finder	fandt	har fundet
at flyve *(to fly)*	flyver	fløj	har fløjet
at få *(to get)*	får	fik	har fået
at give *(to give)*	giver	gav	har givet
at gå *(to walk)*	går	gik	er/har gået
at have *(to have)*	har	havde	har haft
at hedde *(to be called)*	hedder	hed	har heddet
at hjælpe *(to help)*	hjælper	hjalp	har hjulpet
at holde *(to hold)*	holder	holdt	har holdt
at komme *(to come)*	kommer	kom	er kommet
at kunne *(modal verb)*	kan	kunne	har kunnet

at løbe *(to run)*	løber	løb	har løbet
at måtte *(modal verb)*	må	måtte	har måttet
at nyde *(to enjoy)*	nyder	nød	har nydt
at tage *(to take)*	tager	tog	har taget
at se *(to see)*	ser	så	har set
at sidde *(to sit)*	sidder	sad	har siddet
at sige *(to say)*	siger	sagde	har sagt
at skulle *(modal verb)*	skal	skulle	har skullet
at sove *(to sleep)*	sover	sov	har sovet
at spørge *(to ask)*	spørger	spurgte	har spurgt
at synge *(to sing)*	synger	sang	har sunget
at sælge *(to sell)*	sælger	solgte	har solgt
at vide *(to know)*	ved	vidste	har vidst
at ville *(modal verb)*	vil	ville	har villet
at vinde *(to win)*	vinder	vandt	har vundet
at være *(to be)*	er	var	har været

For the translation of modal verbs please refer to Unit 4.

 Practice

1 Fill in the gaps in the table with the correct version of each verb.

Infinitiv	Nutid	Datid	Førnutid	Førdatid
at læse	læser	læste	har læst	havde læst
	snakker			
			har købt	
				havde arbejdet
at være				
		spiste		
at bo				
	har			

2 Complete the sentences with the Danish translation of the word in brackets in the correct tense.

a Igår _____ Jens på arbejde. *(cycle)*

b Oskar _____ i København siden 2009. *(work)*

c Jeg _____ med Ditte i sidste uge. *(talk)*

d De _____ os igår. *(visit)*

e Vi _____ venner i 12 år. *(be)*

f Jeg _____ meget i Kina. *(travel)*

3 Translate the following statements into Danish.

   a I don't like salmon.
   b I prefer Danish films.
   c I like walking.
   d I would rather walk than drive.

Conversation 2

07.04 A teacher is talking to her class about the political parties in Denmark.

1 How many parties are mentioned?

Lærer	Hvem kan nævne partier som ligger til venstre?
Elev 1	Der er Enhedslisten, Socialistisk Folkeparti og Socialdemokratiet.
Lærer	Ja, og hvilke partier ligger til højre?
Elev 2	Der er de konservative, Venstre, Dansk Folkeparti og Liberal alliance.
Elev 1	Hvorfor hedder de Venstre, hvis de ligger til højre?
Lærer	Da Folketinget først blev oprettet var der kun 2 grupper i Folketinget, og de hed højre og venstre. Senere kom Socialdemokratiet til, men det oprindelige venstre navn bruges stadig af partiet Venstre, selvom de er liberale.
Elev 1	Er Det Radikale Venstre så heller ikke radikalt?
Lærer	Nej, de er i midten.

2 Where did Venstre get its name from?

3 Is Det Radikal Venstre to the left or the right on the political spectrum?

Reading

Read this item from the newspaper and answer the questions.

Igår vandt forfatteren Signe Jensen den danske litteraturpris 'De Gyldne Laurbær' for bogen 'Røde tomater'. Hun udtalte at hun var meget glad for prisen og at hendes mand havde købt champagne for at fejre det . Signe Jensen blev født i Horsens i 1968, hvor hun boede indtil 1987. Hun læste filosofi på Københavns Universitet fra 1987–1992. I 2 år boede hun i Tyskland, før hun flyttede tilbage til Danmark. Hun har boet i Ribe siden

2001 sammen med sin mand. Hendes første bog udkom i 1998. 'Røde Tomater' er hendes sjette bog.

1 **What happened yesterday?**
2 **Has Signe Jensen always lived in Denmark?**
3 **What verb is used in Danish for** *to study*?
4 **How many books has Signe Jensen written?**

Writing

Valdemar is a politician who has to write a short synopsis of his life for a website entry. Write it for him including the following information.

> 1984: Born in Slagelse
> 1990: Moved to Korsør
> 2002–2007: Studied Maths at Aarhus University
> 2007–2013: Worked as a teacher in Herfølge
> Since 2014: Member of Parliament
> Lives in Herfølge with his wife and two children.

Speaking

Imagine you are meeting someone in Denmark for the first time. Give a short summary of your life, for example, tell them where you have lived and where you have worked.

Pronunciation

07.05 Here are a few words which have all appeared in this book. Listen to the pronunciation and then repeat them. Pay particular attention to the 's', 'd', 'r' and 'y' sounds. Remember you can find help on pronunciation in the guide at the front of the book.

rød	syvende	dyret	gade
snakke	øre	lærer	læge

? Test yourself

1 Translate the following sentences to Danish.
   a Johan talked to Birgitte yesterday.
   b He has studied English for four years.
   c Last month I read three books.
   d We have lived in Denmark since 2010.

2 Complete the sentences below.
   a Jeg _____ i Danmark i 12 år.
   b Hun _____ i England da hun var barn. (bo)
   c I sidste måned _____ vi en ny bil. (købe)
   d Han _____ mange bøger. (læse)
   e Igår _____ jeg kaffe. (drikke)
   f De _____ meget i Kina. (rejse)

3 How would you say the following in Danish?
   a I love tomatoes.
   b I prefer rice to pasta.
   c I don't like beer.

SELF CHECK

I CAN ...
. . . use verbs in different past tenses.
. . . express likes and dislikes.

8 *Dansk mad*
Danish food

In this unit you will learn how to:
▶ *talk about food in Denmark.*
▶ *use the passive form of verbs.*
▶ *compare adjectives.*
▶ *thank someone appropriately.*

CEFR: (A1) *Can follow short, simple written directions (e.g. go from X to Y).*
(A2) *Can use simple descriptive language to make brief statements about and compare objects and possessions.*

Dansk frokost

A Danish family **frokost** (*lunch*) can be a long and slightly complicated affair. It is not a three-course meal but a collection of various dishes, most of them eaten with **rugbrød** (*rye bread*) or sometimes **franskbrød** (*white bread*). The first dish is the fish, most often pickled **sild** (*herring*) in various flavours, but other fish can be included as well. This is followed by warm dishes such as **frikadeller** (*meatballs*), **flæskesteg** (*roast pork*) or **leverpostej** (*liver pâté*) served with **rødkål** (*red cabbage*) or **agurkesalat** (*cucumber salad*). Next are the cold meats such as **skinke** (*ham*), **spegepølse** (*salami*) or **rullepølse** (type of sausage), which normally take different toppings like **mayonnaise, remoulade** or **ristede løg** (*onion crispies*). This is followed by **ost** (*cheese*). You often drink **øl** and **snaps** (this is a strong spirit, not to be confused with schnaps). There are regional differences and variations between families, but it is always a social thing and can last for hours!

Look at the words in bold above. What do you think the Danish words are for 'sausage' and 'bread'?

In Denmark you are normally expected to serve yourself at the table; do not expect a full plate of food to be put in front of you.

Vocabulary builder

Look at the words and fill in the missing translations. Then listen and try to imitate the pronunciation of the speakers.

FOOD

smør (-ret)	*butter*
hjemmelavet	*homemade*
hurtig	*fast*
nem	*easy*
sund	*healthy*
at piske	*to whip*
at røre	*to stir*
sulten	*hungry*
mæt	*full (had enough to eat)*
at smage	*to taste*
en tallerken (-er)	*a plate*
en kniv(-e)	_____
en gaffel(-er)	*a fork*
en ske (-er)	*a spoon*

NEW EXPRESSIONS

Vil du række mig …?	*Could you pass me …., please?*
Undskyld jeg rækker over	*Sorry for reaching across*
Værsgo	*Here you go*

Conversation 1

08.02 *The Jensen family are gathered for a traditional lunch.*

1 What food is on the table?

Bjørn	Vil du række mig leverpostejen.
Birgitte	Ja, værsgo.
Bjørn	Mm, den er god, er den hjemmelavet?
Birgitte	Nej, men jeg synes faktisk den her er bedre end en hjemmelavet.
Adam	Ja, den er da hurtigere at lave.
Birgitte	Ja, hurtigere og nemmere.
Kamilla	Undskyld jeg rækker over, jeg tager lige noget rugbrød.

Birgitte	Selvfølgelig. Skal jeg sende spegepølsen og remouladen ned til dig også?
Kamilla	Nej ellers tak – jeg tager rullepølsen i stedet for.
Adam	Skal vi have en snaps til?
Bjørn	Ja, tak – selv om det nok ikke er sundt.
Adam	Lidt snaps ind imellem er da fint nok.
Kamilla	Ja, vand er sundest, men en snaps er også god.
Adam	Skål!
Kamilla	Skål!
Bjørn	Skal!
Birgitte	Skal!

2 What do you think 'ellers tak' means?

3 What is the Danish word for *cheers***?**

4 Find the words for *quick* **and** *healthy***. What do you notice?**

 # Language discovery

1 COMPARATIVE AND SUPERLATIVE FORMS OF ADJECTIVES

Adjectives can be used to make comparisons (*Peter is taller than Simon*). That is the comparative form, and in Danish that form ends in **-ere**. For example: **Januar er koldere end juli**. (January is colder than July)

Adjectives can also be used to say that something is *the longest*, *shortest*, *best* and so on. That is the superlative form. In Danish that form ends in **-est** or **-st**.

Here are some examples of adjectives in the basic form, comparative and superlative:

varm, varmere, varmest

nem, nemmere, nemmest

sund, sundere, sundest

hurtig, hurtigere, hurtigst

For adjectives that are very long, the comparative and superlative are usually made by using **mere** and **mest**:

interessant, mere interessant, mest interessant

intelligent, mere intelligent, mest intelligent

(This is just like in English, for example, *more interesting*, *most interesting*.)

There are some irregular adjectives that change vowels in the comparative/ superlative, and a few change completely. For example:

god, bedre, bedst

gammel, ældre, ældst

ung, yngre, yngst

stor, større, størst

lille, mindre, mindst

(Again the same thing happens in English, for example, *good, better, best*.)

2 VERBS IN THE PASSIVE FORM

The passive can be used to describe something happening to something or someone, as opposed to somebody actively doing it. Or you could say that passive is used to turn an object of a sentence into the subject. For example, **Maden spises af drengen** (*The food is eaten by the boy*) is passive whereas **Drengen spiser maden** (*The boy eats the food*) is active.

In Danish this form can be created in two different ways.

By adding **-s** to the infinitive:

Stearinlys tændes ofte i kirken.	*Candles are often lit in the church.*
Æggehviderne piskes til de er stive.	*The egg whites are whisked until stiff.*
Sild spises ofte i Danmark.	*Herring are eaten often in Denmark.*

By combining the verb with **at blive**:

Stearinlys bliver ofte tændt i kirken.	*Candles are often lit in the church.*
Cykler bliver stjålet hver dag.	*Bikes are stolen every day.*
Bøfferne blev stegt for længe.	*The steaks were fried too long.*

Note: we are using the same form of the verb as for **førnutid** (see Unit 7).

3 TAK

08.03 Danish has many different ways of saying *thank you*, some of which have already been covered.

Mange tak	*Thanks a lot*
Tusind tak	*A thousand thanks*
Ellers tak	*Thanks, but no thanks*
Tak skal du have	*Thank you to you*

Selv tak	*Thank you yourself* (This is a response if somebody has thanked you, but you feel they had equal input.)
Tak i lige måde	*Thank you to you as well* (Again a reply if somebody is thanking you and you also want to thank them)
Tak for idag	*Thank you for today*
Tak for sidst	*Thank you for last time* (You say that the next time you see a person following a party/event, etc. It is a way of saying that you enjoyed yourself.)
Tak for lån	*Thank you for letting me borrow it* (This is used when returning an item you have borrowed.)
Tak for mad	*Thank you for the meal* (You should always say this at the end of meal to the host/the person who cooked the meal. The reply is 'velbekomme'.)
Tak for hjælpen	*Thank you for your help*
Tak for ...	*Thank you for ...* (Danes are often quite specific when giving thanks, so you will often hear **Tak for** followed by something.)

Practice

1 Translate these sentences into Danish.

   a John is older than Carl.

   b Sarah is fastest, but Anna is the most intelligent.

   c Water is healthier than wine.

   d A car is fast, but a train is faster.

   e Peter is smaller than Hans, but Leo is smallest.

2 Complete the sentence by putting the verb in brackets in the passive form.

   a Bøfferne _____ på panden. (at stege)

   b Huset skal _____ til sommer. (at male)

   c Tasker _____ hver dag på togstationen. (at stjæle)

   d Fløden _____ til flødeskum. (at piske)

   e Jordbær _____ mest om sommeren. (at spise)

3 Match a statement from the first column with an answer from the second.

a	Tak for lån af bogen.	**1**	Tak i lige måde.
b	Tak for sidst.	**2**	Velbekomme.
c	Tak for mad.	**3**	Det var så lidt.
d	Tak for idag.	**4**	Kunne du lide den?
e	Tak for hjælpen.	**5**	Selv tak.

Conversation 2

08.04 *Adam and Bjørn run into each other at the train station a few days after the lunch.*

1 What did Bjørn give Adam at the lunch?

Bjørn	Hej Adam – tak for sidst.
Adam	Selv tak, det var en hyggelig eftermiddag.
Bjørn	Ja, det var det – og en masse dejlig mad.
Adam	Vi fik nok at spise, og tak for snapsen forøvrigt, hjemmelavet dildsnaps er skønt.
Bjørn	Det var så lidt.
Adam:	Her kommer mit tog, jeg må på arbejde. Vi ses.
Bjørn	Hej, hej.

2 Which expression indicates that Adam enjoyed himself?

3 How do we know there was lots of food at the lunch?

Reading

Read the following recipe for a dessert Danes eat at Christmas and then answer the questions.

Risalamande

1½ dl vand	1 spsk sukker
1½ dl grødris	1 tsk vaniljesukker
5 dl mælk	25 g mandler
2 dl piskefløde	

Vandet bringes i kog og grødrisene hældes i. Risene koges i få minutter, hvorefter mælken tilsættes. Mælken bringes i kog under omrøring og koges under omrøring indtil risengrøden har en ensartet konsistens. Grøden afkøles.

Mandlerne skoldes og hakkes. Fløden piskes til flødeskum. Bland risengrøden med piskefløden, mandlerne, sukker og vaniliesukker.

Risalamanden serveres med varm kirsebærsovs

a   What are the main ingredients?
b   Is **risalamande** served warm or cold?
c   What is served with **risalamande**?
d   Recipes often use two different forms of the verbs. Which ones
    are they?

Writing

**You have been to a dinner party at a friend's house. Write them a
short note or email to thank them for the evening, expressing that
you had a lovely time.**

Speaking

 08.05 Play the part of Tove in the dialogue.

Tove	*(May I have the butter please?)*
Ditte	Værsgo.
Tove	*(Will you pass me the salami as well please?)*
Ditte	Ja, selvfølgelig.
Tove	*(Thank you to you. The food is lovely.)*
Ditte	Tak! Så skal vi vist sige skål.
Tove	*(Cheers.)*

> When listening to a group of Danes talking, for example, at a lunch, you might notice a
> few English words popping up. Many English words have been adopted into the
> Danish language, particularly in business and IT, but also unfortunately several English
> language swear words. Please be aware that these words do not carry the same
> weight to a Dane as they would to an English speaker; the words are primarily used to
> emphasize rather than to offend. Because of their common use in Danish they also
> often appear when Danes are speaking English. Please don't feel too upset, the Danes
> generally do not realize how offensive the words are!

Test yourself

1 Fill in the gaps in the table using the comparative and superlative forms of the adjectives.

hurtig	hurtigere	hurtigst
stor		
	sødere	
nem		
		mindst
dejlig		

2 Translate the sentences into Danish.
- **a** Many bikes are stolen every day.
- **b** The cake is served with cream.
- **c** The food is eaten by the dog.

3 What would you say in the following situations?
- **a** At the end of a meal
- **b** When you meet a friend you last saw at a party
- **c** When returning a book you have borrowed

4 If sitting at the table how would you:
- **a** ask for the sugar?
- **b** ask for somebody to pass you the butter?

SELF CHECK

I CAN ...
. . . talk about food in Denmark.
. . . use the passive form of verbs.
. . . compare adjectives.
. . . thank someone appropriately.

9 Fritid

Spare time

In this unit you will learn how to:
▶ *talk about hobbies and sport.*
▶ *express opinions.*
▶ *use reflexive pronouns.*
▶ *use relative pronouns.*

CEFR: (A2) *Can use simple descriptive language to make brief statements about and compare objects and possessions. Can take a short, simple message. Can make and respond to suggestions. Can write about past events.*

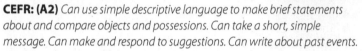

Sport in Denmark

The two most popular sports in Denmark are **fodbold** (*football*) and **håndbold** (*handball*). The Danish football team is popular, although not always hugely successful, and the Danes still like to remember that Denmark won **EM** or **Europa Mesterskaberne** (*European Championships*) in football in 1992. Handball is very popular and both the men's and women's teams have won several medals and championships. Other popular sports in Denmark include badminton, tennis, **cykelsport** (*cycling*), **svømning** (*swimming*), golf and **sejlsport** (*sailing*).

Thinking about what EM stands for, what do you think DM and VM stand for?

Vocabulary builder

09.01 Look at the words and phrases and complete the missing English expressions. Then listen and try to imitate the pronunciation of the speakers.

SPORTS

at vinde	_____
at tabe	*to lose*
at score	_____
et mål (-)	*a goal*
første halvleg	*first half*
anden halvleg	*second half*
uafgjort	*a draw*
et stadion (-er)	_____
en landskamp (-e)	*international match*
en dommer (-e)	*referee*
en svømmehal (-ler)	*swimming pool*
at spille	*play*
at ride	_____
en bane (-r)	*field/court/pitch/track*

HOBBIES

skak	*chess*
samle på	*to collect*
et frimærke (-r)	*stamp*
en mønt (-er)	*coin*
en biograf (-er)	*cinema*
gå en tur	*go for a walk*

The English word *to play* has two translations in Danish. **At spille** is what you do if there are set rules or systems in place, for example, **spille fodbold**, **spille skak** or even **spille guitar** (or any other musical instrument). **At lege** is used for talking about imaginative or pretend play (think of building blocks).

Conversation 1

09.02 *Signe and Sara are talking about what to do at the weekend.*

1 What options are presented?

Signe	Jeg synes vi skal tage i biografen, jeg vil gerne se Susanne Biers nye film.
Sara	Nej, det gider jeg ikke – jeg er ikke så vild med Susanne Bier.
Signe	Jeg tror den er rigtig god – det synes jeg altid hendes film er.
Sara	Vi kunne tage i svømmehallen? Eller Jens spurgte om vi ville med til landskampen i Parken?
Signe	Nej fodbold har jeg ikke lyst til! Det er kedeligt – vi skal ud og more os.
Sara	Vi kunne tage i Tivoli og hygge os?
Signe	Ja, Tivoli lyder som en god ide – jeg tror der er koncert derinde på lørdag.
Sara	Ja, en koncert ville være alletiders – det synes jeg vi skal gøre.

2 Why doesn't Sara want to go to the cinema?

3 What is Signe's opinion of football?

4 How many verbs can you find that are used to express an opinion?

5 Find expressions for *having fun* **and** *having a nice time*.

 # Language discovery

1 RELATIVE PRONOUNS

Relative pronouns are the words used to link clauses together. In English we use *who*, *which* or *that*, for example, *It was John who made the dinner* or *Elsa has a dress that is green*. In English the relative pronoun is decided by what is being referred back to, for example, *who* would be used when referring back to a person. In Danish the relative pronoun is dependent on whether it is referring back to the subject of the sentence or not.

The two main relative pronouns in Danish are **som** and **der**. They always relate to the noun immediately preceding them.

Det var Johan, som lavede maden. *It was Johan who made the dinner.*
Det var Johan, der lavede maden.

Else har en kjole, der er grøn. *Else has a dress that is green.*
Else har en kjole, som er grøn.

In both these sentences the relative pronoun represents the subject and therefore **som** and **der** are interchangeable and you can use either.

Her er bogen, som jeg læste. *Here is the book that I read.*

Here the relative pronoun represents the object and therefore only **som** can be used.

As in English the relative pronoun can usually be left out if it is not the subject.

Her er bogen jeg læste. *Here is the book I read.*

2 REFLEXIVE PRONOUNS

A reflexive pronoun refers back to the subject of the sentence; it indicates that the subject is doing something that involves themselves.

Jeg slog mig. *I hurt myself.*

Katten slikkede sig. *The cat licked itself.*

In Danish there are more verbs that take a reflexive pronoun than in English.

The reflexive pronouns are:

mig	**Jeg vaskede mig.**	*I washed myself.*
dig	**Du skyndte dig.**	*You hurried yourself up.*
sig	**Han barberede sig.**	*He shaved.*
	Hun skar sig.	*She cut herself.*
	Den satte sig.	*It sat down.*
os	**Vi hyggede os.**	*We enjoyed ourselves.*
jer	**I keder jer.**	*You are bored.*
sig	**De morer sig.**	*They are having a good time.*

3 EXPRESSING OPINIONS

Here are some of the most common expressions used to give your opinion.

Jeg tror *I believe*

Jeg synes *I think*

Jeg mener   *It is my opinion/I think*

Jeg er overbevist om …   *I am convinced that …*

In a dictionary *to think* will often be translated as **at tænke**. This is to think in the sense of using your brain, for example, **Jeg tænker på dig hele tiden** (*I am thinking about you all the time*).

Practice

1 Som can be used in all of the following sentences, but only three of them can use der. Can you spot which ones?

   a Her er den bil _____ vi vil købe.

   b I parken er der en dreng _____ spiller fodbold.

   c Pigen, _____ hedder Amalie, er meget god til håndbold.

   d Den kage _____ jeg fik smagte ikke godt.

   e Der er 5 personer _____ snakker på samme tid.

2 Insert the correct reflexive pronoun.

   a De skyndte _____ at køre til stadion for at se fodbold.

   b Jeg keder _____ altid til fodboldkampe.

   c Han slog _____ på døren.

   d Du kan sætte _____ i den blå stol.

   e Vi morede _____ i biografen.

   f Hun vaskede _____ hver morgen.

3 Translate the following into Danish.

   a I think it is a good idea.

   b I believe there is a concert tomorrow.

   c What do you think?

   d I am convinced the sun will shine tomorrow.

Reading

Read this football report and answer the questions.

Det blev uafgjort igår mellem FC Midtjylland og FC København i søndagens superliga opgør. FC Midtjylland lagde stærkt ud med et mål efter kun 10 minutter, men FC København var hurtigt med og udlignede til 1–1 efter 27 minutter. I anden halvleg var det FC København som scorede først og 10 minutter senere var det endda lige ved at blive 3–1, men FC Midtjylland blev ved med at lægge pres på sjællænderne og 5 minutter før tid udlignede de og sikrede sig det ene point med 2–2 resultatet.

OB vandt en 1–0 sejr over Aab på hjemmebane i Odense, mens Esbjerg tabte 1–3 til Brøndby. Esbjerg fik en spiller udvist efter kun 20 minutter, og kunne med kun 10 spillere ikke hamle op med et velspillende Brøndby hold.

   a How many matches are mentioned?
   b Who won each match?
   c What is the Danish word for *equalize*?
   d What happened to the Esbjerg team?

Writing

Look back at the report about the football matches, then write a short summary of a sports match you have seen (or find a description of one on the internet you can pretend to have seen).

The Danish word **først** can have two meanings, unlike the English *first*. **Først** can mean either *in the beginning of* or *not until*. For example, the sentence **Da jeg først fik børn var jeg meget træt** translates as *When I first had children I was very tired*, but **Det var først da jeg fik børn at jeg blev meget træt** translates as *It wasn't until I had children I became tired*. Normally you will know from the context what is meant.

Conversation 2

 09.05 *Sanne is phoning Gitte to arrange an evening out. It is Jesper who answers the phone.*

1 Is Gitte home?

Jesper	Ja, det er Jesper.
Sanne	Hej Jesper, det er Sanne. Er Gitte hjemme?
Jesper	Nej, hun er lige gået en tur. Vil du ringe senere eller kan jeg give hende en besked?
Sanne	Vil du sige til hende at jeg henter hende klokken 6 i aften.
Jesper	Ja selvfølgelig – klokken 6 i aften.
Sanne	Jeg kunne også bare sende en sms, det er nok nemmere.
Jesper	Det er ikke noget problem, jeg skal nok give beskeden videre.
Sanne	Og sig at hun skal huske gaven til Matilde.
Jesper	OK – husk gaven til Matilde. Er der andet?
Sanne	Nej det var det. Tak skal du have. Hej, hej.
Jesper	Hej, hej.

2 What is the Danish expression for *taking a message***?**

3 How would you say *I will pass on the message***?**

4 How would you say *anything else***?**

> Danes usually say their name when they answer the phone. **Hallo** is not really a greeting in Danish; it is often an indication that you can't quite hear the person you are talking to.

Speaking

09.06 Erik is arriving at the office. Maria is at the reception desk. Play the part of Erik in this conversation.

Maria	Hej Erik, jeg har en besked til dig fra Simon.
Erik	*(Yes, what is it?)*
Maria	Han kommer og henter dig klokken 3.
Erik	*(Simon is coming at 3 o'clock. Anything else?)*
Maria	Ja, du skal huske at tænde for din mobiltelefon.
Erik	*(Ha ha, thank you. See you later.)*
Maria	Hej hej.

Writing

Christian has called and asked you to leave a message for Sofie saying that he will pick her up at 7.30 to go to the cinema. Sofie also needs to remember to bring Christian's scarf. Write the message for Sofie.

Pronunciation

1 09.07 Here are a few words which have all appeared in this book. Listen to the pronunciation and then repeat them. Pay particular attention to the t, tt, kk, pp sounds. Remember you can find help on pronunciation in the guide at the front of the book.

> Mette   hente   det   ikke   kniv
> sukker   Jeppe   sætte   kendte

2 09.08 The following text is about Danish film directors. Try to read the text out loud, then listen carefully to the pronunciation and repeat it again. Remember the quite flat intonation of Danish and remember that an -e at the end of a word cannot be ignored!

Der er flere kendte danske filminstruktører, som har lavet film på både dansk og engelsk. Lars von Trier har lavet flere kontroversielle film, Lone Scherfig blev nomineret til en Oscar for filmen *An Education* og Nikolas Winding Refn vandt prisen for bedste instruktør i Cannes for filmen *Drive*.

?⃞ Test yourself

1 Translate into Danish.

   a He shaves every morning.

   b We are bored.

   c Sit down!

   d I am having fun.

   e They hurried to school.

2 Insert a relative pronoun.

   a Her er min hund _____ hedder Bingo.

   b Her er bogen _____ jeg skrev.

   c Det er min computer _____ er gået istykker.

   d Har du set filmèn _____ går i biografen?

   e Vis mig kjolen _____ du købte.

3 How would you say the following in Danish?

   a I think it is a good idea.

   b I think the jacket is very expensive.

   c I believe we have to turn right.

   d I think he is 20 years old.

SELF CHECK

I CAN ...

- ... talk about hobbies and sport.
- ... express opinions.
- ... use reflexive pronouns.
- ... use relative pronouns.

10 *Højtider og familiefester*

Holidays and family celebrations

In this unit you will learn to:
▸ *talk about Danish holidays.*
▸ *talk about common family events.*
▸ *use uncountable nouns.*
▸ *use demonstrative pronouns.*
▸ *use* some *or* any.

CEFR: (A2) *Can identify the main points of news items. Can understand short, simple personal letters. Can write very simple, personal letter.*

Holidays

Danish holidays are generally linked to the Christian calendar, so throughout the year the following days are considered public holidays: **skærtorsdag** (*Maundy Thursday*), **langfredag** (*Good Friday*), **påskedag** (*Easter Sunday*), **2. påskedag** (*Easter Monday*), **Kristi himmelfarts dag** (*Ascension*), **pinsedag** (*Whitsun*), **2. pinsedag, juleaften** (*Christmas Eve*), **juledag** (*Christmas Day*), **2. juledag** (*26th December*), **nytårsdag** (*New Year's Day*). The fourth Friday after Easter is also a holiday known as **store Bededag** (*Prayer Day*). The only other public holiday is the 5th June, which is **grundlovsdag** (*Constitution Day*), where a lot of people will get half a day off work. **Fastelavn** (*Shrovetide*) is also celebrated widely by dressing up and eating **fastelavnsboller**, but it is not a holiday.

Christmas is primarily celebrated **juleaften**, which is when the Danes open **julegaver** and walk around the **juletræ** while singing **julesange**.

Thinking of some of the Danish words you have learned in other units, what do you think these are: **julekalender**, **julefrokost** and **julemand**?

Vocabulary builder

10.01 Look at the words and phrases and complete the missing English expressions. Then listen and try to imitate the pronunciation of the speakers.

CELEBRATIONS

at fejre	*to celebrate*
en barnedåb (-e)	*christening*
en fødselsdag(-e)	*birthday*
en konfirmation (-er)	_____
et bryllup(-per)	*wedding*
en bryllupsdag(-e)	*anniversary*
et sølvbryllup	_____
et guldbryllup	_____

NEW EXPRESSIONS

Glædelig jul	*Merry Christmas*
Godt nytår	*Happy New Year*
God påske	*Happy Easter*
God pinse	*Happy Whitsun*
Tillykke med fødselsdagen	*Happy birthday*
Tillykke med brylluppet	*Congratulations on your wedding day*
Tillykke med …	*Congratulations on …*

> Danes celebrate twelve and a half years of marriage (half way to 25!). It is known as **kobberbryllup**, and is often a big celebration.

Conversation 1

 10.02 *Jan and Lone have just celebrated their 25th anniversary. It is the day after the big party and they are talking about the evening's events.*

1 What presents did they receive?

Jan	Det var en god aften igår!
Lone	Ja, det var bare så hyggeligt, og der var nogle rigtig gode sange og taler.
Jan	Ja, den sang fra Bo og Sidse var så sjov.
Lone	Og sikke mange gaver – lad os gå ind og se på dem igen.
Jan	Den her kasse vin fra alle naboerne glæder jeg mig til at åbne.
Lone	De her Georg Jensen lysestager er super flotte – meget klassiske.
Jan	Dansk design er altid godt. Der er også en Kähler vase.
Lone	Ja, og en ny Stelton kaffekande.
Jan	Hm, jeg kunne faktisk godt drikke en kop kaffe lige nu. Vil du have noget kaffe?
Lone	Ja tak, der er vist også nogle kager tilbage.
Jan	Er der flere af de der røde kager for de smagte rigtig godt?
Lone	Nej, jeg tror ikke der er nogen, men kig i køkkenet.

2 Find three words in the dialogue that could be translated as
some **or** *any***.**

3 Looking at the dialogue, how do you think *den her* **and** *de der* **would translate into English?**

> At any kind of celebration it is common for guests to write songs about the person or couple being celebrated. It will simply be new words to a well-known tune and all guests will sing it together.

Language discovery

1 DEMONSTRATIVE PRONOUNS

In English the demonstrative pronouns are *this*, *that*, *these* and *those*.

In Danish the demonstrative pronouns tend to take different forms in writing and in speaking. As in so many other instances, which pronoun you use depends on whether it is relating to an **'en'** word or a **'et'** word.

Written form	Spoken form	
Denne bil er sort.**Dette** hus er stort.	**Den her** bil er sort.**Det her** hus er stort.	*This car is black.This house is big.*
Den bil er sort.**Det** hus er stort.	**Den der** bil er sort.**Det der** hus er stort.	*That car is black.That house is big.*
Disse huse er gule.	**De her** huse er gule.	*These houses are yellow.*
De der huse er røde.	**De der** huse er røde.	*Those houses are red.*

2 UNCOUNTABLE NOUNS

In English there are many uncountable nouns, for example, *money*, *furniture*, *wages*, *milk*, *water*, *information*. Most of them are considered singular, but a few are plural, such as *wages*, *contents* and *scissors*.

Danish has uncountable nouns as well, but they are not always the same as in English and the distinction between singular and plural can also differ. For example, in English the word *money* is singular, but in Danish the word **penge** is plural.

In both English and Danish it is possible to quantify an uncountable noun by using a different noun, for example, a piece of furniture or a glass of milk. In Danish you could use nouns such as **et stykke** (*a piece*), **et glas**, **en kop**, **en portion**.

Here is a list of some uncountable nouns in Danish, both in the indefinite and definite form as this will also tell you if they are singular or plural. (Remember the definite endings of nouns from Unit 2.)

penge/pengene (*money*)
kontanter/kontanterne (*cash*)
løn/lønnen (*wages*)
tøj/tøjet (*clothes*)
mælk/mælken
ris/risene

vand/vandet
musik/musikken
mad/maden (*food*)
kaffe/kaffen
fløde/fløden (*cream*)
smørrebrød/smørrebrødet

Note: these words are not uncountable in Danish: **en saks** (*scissors*), **en oplysning** (*information*).

3 SOME AND ANY

Nogen, **noget** and **nogle** are the equivalents of *some* or *any*.

Nogen is used:

▶ about people – **Er der nogen hjemme?** (*Anybody home?*)

▶ in a sentence with **ikke** or **aldrig** in front of an **-n** word – **Jeg har ikke nogen ordbog (en ordbog).** (*I don't have a (any) dictionary.*)

▶ in a sentence with **ikke eller aldrig** in front of plural – **Jeg har ikke nogen bøger.** (*I don't have any books.*)

Noget is used:

▶ about things/something generally undefined – **Vil du hjæpe mig med noget?** (*Will you help me with something?*)

▶ in front of an uncountable noun in the singular, or if the uncountable noun is implied – **Har du noget mælk? Nej, jeg har ikke noget.** (*Do you have any milk? No, I don't have any.*)

▶ in a sentence with **ikke eller aldrig** in front of a **t**-word – **Ulla har ikke noget arbejde (et arbejde).** (*Ulla doesn't have a (any) job.*)

Nogle is used:

▶ in front of plural – **Lise købte nogle kager.** (*Lise bought some cakes.*)

> **Nogle** is pronounced in exactly the same way as **nogen**, so only in writing will you notice a difference.

 Practice

1 Translate these sentences into Danish.
   a This sofa is red.
   b That tree is very tall.
   c These cats are white, but those are black.
   d This book is long.

2 Countable or uncountable? Do the sentences need en/et in the gap or not? If they do, add it.

a Jeg sender _____ postkort til dig.

b Lene drikker ikke _____ mælk.

c Har du _____ saks?

d Vil du have _____ rødvin?

e Husk at drikke _____ vand.

f Jeg har _____ kusine, der bor på Samsø.

3 Insert nogen, noget or nogle.

a Har du _____ kaffe?

b Lotte har _____ problemer med sin cykel.

c Han har ikke _____ penge.

d Kender du _____ i Korsør.

e Hun skal hjælpe ham med _____.

f Der kom ikke _____ bus.

Listening

10.03 Try listening to this news item before looking at the text. Then answer the questions.

> Tivoli i København vil i år for første gang holde åbent juleaftensdag. Julemarkedet i Tivoli åbner d.15. november, og denne gang vil der også være åbent juleaftensdag. Tivoli håber at den ekstra dag vil appellere både til turister i byen og til dem som ikke fejrer julen på traditional dansk vis. De tror også der vil være børnefamilier som gerne vil bruge et par timer af den lange ventetid inden juleaften i Tivoli. Allerede for et par år siden blev åbningstiderne udvidet til nytårsaftensdag og det er håbet at juleaftensdag kan blive en lige så stor success og dermed en fast tradition.

a What is the news story about?

b Who do they expect will make use of this new opportunity?

c Is this an opportunity for one year only?

Reading

Emilie has just had her konfirmation. She sends a letter to her aunt abroad who could not attend the celebrations telling her about the day. Read the letter and answer the questions.

Kære Susan,

Tusind tak for gaven til min konfirmation - jeg har uret på hver dag. Jeg havde en rigtig dejlig dag, hvor solen skinnede. Der var mange mennesker i kirken om morgenen, og bagefter var der 40 mennesker til middag. Næsten alle fra familien var der, vi savnede bare dig og så min fars bror Nikolaj. Jeg fik masser af gaver. Der var nogle flotte smykker, og en ny ipad og så 10.000kr. Jeg har ikke besluttet hvad jeg skal bruge dem til endnu. Dagen var bare så hyggelig! Jeg skal nok sende nogle billeder til dig.

Håber du snart kommer til Danmark.

Kærlig hilsen

Emilie

a Did she enjoy the day?
b What presents did Emilie get?
c Who could not make it to the party?

All Danes are automatically a member of the *Danish State Church* (**Folkekirken**) unless they specifically choose to opt out. So while many religious celebrations are still upheld, for example, the majority of Danish children have a confirmation, they often place more emphasis on the family element of this than the religious element.

Writing

Signe and Martin are getting married. They have sent you this invitation.

Kære XXX og XXX

Vi skal giftes og det ville glæde os meget, hvis I vil være med til at fejre dagen.

Vielsen finder sted i Ansgar Kirke i Odense lørdag d. 16. maj, kl. 14

Bagefter vil vi gerne invitere til kaffe og kage, efterfulgt af middag og dans i Hjallese Forsamlingshus.

Vi glæder os til at se jer.

Kærlig hilsen

Signe og Martin

S.U. senest 25. april

Reply to Signe and Martin accepting the invitation. You could include expressions such as vil gerne komme or glæde sig til or you can use other expressions you have learned in the book.

 Speaking

You are at a friend's birthday party. Make this short speech in Danish to congratulate him:

> Dear Jesper. This day is a good day. It is the day we celebrate a man who is very funny, very clever and a very good friend. I would like to say happy birthday and I look forward to many more years with you. Happy birthday and cheers!

Pronunciation

 10.04 In the box is the name of a Danish dessert (a kind of stewed fruit with cream). It is known just as much for being hard to pronounce for non-native speakers as for its flavour. Listen to the pronunciation and then repeat.

> **Rødgrød med fløde**

1 Insert the correct demonstrative pronoun. You can choose if you want to use the written or the spoken form.
   a _____ bog er min.
   b _____ huse er meget dyre, men _____ er billigere.
   c _____ træ er gammelt.
   d _____ bil er meget hurtig.

2 Here is a list of words. Which are countable and which are uncountable?

> **Mælk, saks, penge, smørrebrød, musik, oplysning, kjole, tøj, avis**

3 Translate these sentences into Danish.
   a Do you want some tea?
   b I don't have any apples.
   c Will you buy some cakes?
   d She doesn't have any money.
   e Can you help me with something?

SELF CHECK

I CAN ...
○ ... talk about Danish holidays.
○ ... talk about common family events.
○ ... use uncountable nouns.
○ ... use demonstrative pronouns.
○ ... use *some* or *any*.

1 Translate the following sentences into Danish.

a I lived in Odense for five years.

b John read a book yesterday.

c I have lived in Denmark for seven years.

d They have bought a big house.

e She has been a doctor for 15 years.

f They danced all night.

g We have cycled 50 kilometres now.

2 Complete the table.

Adjective	Comparative	Superlative
stor		
	gladere	
		nemmest
	mindre	
gammel		
	hurtigere	
interessant		

3 Insert the verb in the passive form.

a Kagen _____ med flødeskum. (at servere)

b Cykler _____ ofte fra togstationen. (at stjæle)

c Musen _____ af katten. (at spise)

d På fødselsdage _____ flaget. (at hejse)

4 Insert the correct pronoun in the sentences.

a Magnus vasker _____ og barberer _____ hver morgen.

b Vi hyggede _____ i Tivoli igår.

c Jeg morede _____ til festen.

d De skyndte _____ i skole.

e Jeg kan se du keder _____.

5 Match the Danish to the English.

a De her hunde er store.

b Den her bil er sort.

c Den der bil er gul.

d De her huse er store.

e De der huse er små.

1 That car is yellow.

2 Those houses are small.

3 These houses are big.

4 These dogs are big.

5 This car is black.

6 Insert nogen, noget or nogle in these sentences.

a Jeg har ikke _____ penge.

b Vil du have _____ kaffe?

c Har du _____ kontanter?

d Vil du hjælpe mig med _____?

7 Think back to the ways you have learned to say *thank you* in Danish.

a What would you say to a friend who has helped you?

b What would you say at the end of a meal?

c What would you say after spending a day in somebody's company?

8 10.05 Jane and Niels are discussing how to celebrate their anniversary. Listen to their conversation and answer the questions.

Jane	Jeg synes vi bare skal holde en lille fest sammen med familien.
Niels	Jeg synes godt vi kan holde en større fest, jeg elsker fester. Det er sjovere med mange mennesker.
Jane	Ja, men hvem skal vi så invitere?
Niels	Vi kunne invitere alle børnene og børnebørnene, vores venner og naboerne og måske nogle kollegaer.
Jane	Jeg bryder mig ikke så meget om store fester – det ved du jo.
Niels	Ja, men det er da hyggeligt at se dem allesammen.
Jane	Men det bliver mere end 100 mennesker, hvor skal vi holde festen?
Niels	Vi kunne gøre det på et hotel eller i forsamlingshuset.
Jane	Så foretrækker jeg forsamlingshuset, det er mere hyggeligt.
Niels	Det er fint. Jeg ringer og spørger dem hvor meget det koster.
Jane	Så laver jeg en liste over gæsterne vi skal invitere.

a How do they each prefer to celebrate?

b Does Jane like big parties?

c Who does Niels want to invite?

d What tasks are they going to do?

Answer key

UNIT 1
Greetings
Good morning, good day, good afternoon, good evening, good night

Vocabulary builder
Hi/hello; See you later

Conversation 1
1 She is going to Roskilde
2a He is going to Aalborg; **b** He is a doctor; **c** She is a teacher; **d** She is from Spain; **e** She lives in Roskilde

Language discovery
1a Hvad hedder du?; **b** Hvad laver du?
2a Jeg er læge; **b** Jeg er lærer **3** in Danish there is no article in front of the profession
4a bor; **b** kommer; **c** besøge; **d** undervise **5** they all end in 'r'
6a Jeg kommer fra Spanien; **b** dansker

Nationalities and languages
skotte, franskmand, nordmand

Practice
1 a 4; **b** 3; **c** 1; **d** 7; **e** 6; **f** 2; **g** 5
2a Han bor i Boston; **b** Jeg kommer fra England; **c** De besøger Niels; **d** Du taler dansk
3a Jeg hedder …; **b** Jeg bor i …; **c** Jeg kommer fra …; **d** Jeg er …

Conversation 2
1 Mette is an engineer, Sofie is an architect
2a Sofie works in Copenhagen; **b** Yes; **c** Only when she has time; **d** Having a cup of coffee

Speaking
Hej; Jeg hedder…., hvor bor du?; Jeg bor i …

Reading

a Maria er lærer; **b** Hun bor i Roskilde; **c** Hun kommer fra Spanien; **d** Niels er læge; **e** Han holder ferie i Spanien

Writing

1 An example could be: Jeg hedder Dorte, jeg bor i Skotland, men jeg er dansker. Jeg er lærer og jeg taler engelsk og dansk.

2a Jeg er arkitekt i København; **b** Har du tid til en kop kaffe?; **c** Jeg hedder Morten og jeg kommer fra Danmark

Test yourself

1a Godmorgen; **b** Hej; **c** Farvel; **d** Godnat

2a Hvad hedder du?; **b** Hvor bor du?; **c** Hvad laver du?

3a Han møder hende; **b** Vi møder dig; **c** Du møder ham; **d** De møder hende; **e** Jeg møder jer

4a Hun er læge; **b** Vi kommer fra Spanien **c** Jeg hedder Peter og jeg er englænder; **d** Han taler engelsk, dansk og fransk; **e** Hvordan går det?; **f** Maria møder os i toget

UNIT 2
Relatives
farfar

Vocabulary builder
Son; grandchild; partner

Conversation 1
1 Sofie

2a No; **b** 5 (1 kusine, 4 fætre), **c** Jens; **d** 2 children (Claus and Rikke) and 3 grandchildren

3 en, syv, ni, to, tre, fire, tolv, femten, seksten

4 søn – son, sønnen – the son, sønner – sons; kusine – cousin, kusiner – cousins, kusinerne – the cousins

Language discovery
Nouns singular
et billede/billedet, en storesøster/storesøsteren, en kusine/kusinen, en familie/familien, en søn/sønnen, en datter/datteren, et barn/barnet

Nouns plural
The houses, the doctors, the men
fætrene (def), kusinerne (def), fætre (indef), kusiner (indef), sønner (indef), billeder (indef)

Practice

1 to, fire, fem, otte, ti, elleve, tolv, fjorten, seksten, sytten

2

Indefinite	Definite
et bord	bordet
en læge	lægen
en englænder	englænderen
et hus	huset
en kone	konen
et billede	billedet
en søster	søsteren

3a sønner, **b** kusiner, **c** danskere, **d** mænd

4a konerne; **b** familierne, **c** børnene, **d** fætrene

Listening and speaking

a Anne er 7 år; **b** Bente og Vagn bor i Allerød; **c** Charlotte kommer fra England; **d** Simons brødre hedder Lars og Jens; **e** Bente og Vagn har otte børnebørn

Reading

Top row from left to right: Jørgen, Merete, Niels, Lis; middle row from left to right: Jette, Peter, Søren, Mette; bottom row from left to right: Laura, Emil

Test yourself

1a 4; **b** 16; **c** 12; **d** 7; **e** 19; **f** 8; **g** 11

2a Sophie er ni år gammel; **b** Kirsten og Caroline er kusiner; **c** Vi har fem børnebørn; **d** Jeg er gift med Jill

3

Singular indefinite	Singular definite	Plural indefinite	Plural definite
en kone	konen	koner	konerne
et bord	bordet	borde	bordene
en kusine	kusinen	kusiner	kusinerne
en søn	sønnen	sønner	sønnerne
en mand	manden	mænd	mændene
Et barn	barnet	børn	børnene

UNIT 3
Being polite

Thank you for the meal

Vocabulary builder

Steak, chocolate, ice cream, apple juice, red wine

Conversation 1

1 Katrine orders chicken salad, a coke, a latte and a piece of chocolate cake; Louise orders meatballs, potato salad, raspberry fruit juice and strawberry tart with cream

2 Kan jeg få…; Jeg vil gerne bede om…; Jeg vil gerne have…

3 Det var det hele

4 The subject and the verb are inverted

Language discovery

Onsdag (Odin), tirsdag (Tyr), torsdag (Thor), fredag (Frigg)

Word order in a sentence
Verb and subject swap places

Practice

1b Sover Jens?; **c** Spiser Hanne frikadeller?; **d** Har jeg 2 sønner?; **e** Drikker de vin?

2a 54; **b** 81; **c** 43; **d** 36; **e** 99

3d Vi ses på torsdag

4a om onsdagen **b** I søndags

5a Søndag arbejder Louise; **b** På en café spiser Katrine og Louise frokost; **c** Nu kommer tjeneren

Conversation 2

1 Next Wednesday

2 Må vi bede om regningen?; det må vi gøre igen; det kan jeg desværre ikke; søndag skal jeg arbejde; Så må vi prøve i næste uge; Onsdag kan jeg også; Så siger vi det; Næste onsdag spiser vi frokost sammen igen; Her er regningen; Så kommer vi her igen på onsdag!

3 Regningen

4 Lørdag, søndag, tirsdag, onsdag

Speaking

Sofie	Kan jeg få en sandwich med kylling og en kaffe
Sofie	Jeg vil gerne bede om chokoladekage
Sofie	Nej tak, det var det hele

Test yourself

1a syvogtredive; **b** enogfirs; **c** nioghalvtreds; **d** seksogtyve; **e** fireogfyrre

2 Jeg vil gerne bede om frikadeller, kartoffelsalat og en øl

3 Kan jeg få regningen; jeg vil gerne bede om regningen

4a søndag; **b** tirsdag; **c** onsdag; **d** lørdag

5a Mandag arbejder Katrine i Århus; **b** På cafeen spiser Louise chokoladekage; **c** På bordet står der vand

REVIEW 1

1a svigermor; **b** Lene is a teacher, Jesper is an architect; **c** 5 (Sille, Amalie, Lukas and the two boys in France); **d** Sille and Amalie are **kusiner** to the boys, the boys are **fætre** to Sille and Amalie

2 The numbers are: 17, 31, 98, 47, 4, 53, 75, 82, 29, 66

3a en mand; **b** læreren; **c** læger; **d** barnet; **e** børnene; **f** en kone; **g** huse; **h** kyllingerne

4 The correct order is: mandag, tirsdag, onsdag, torsdag, fredag, lørdag, søndag

5a To visit his cousin in Svendborg; **b** Thomas' cousin; **c** To Nyborg to work; **d** They use informal greetings (hej, dav, vi ses, hej, hej)

6a Jesper er arkitekt; **b** Pigen hedder Mette; **c** Han møder hende; **d** Hver mandag går de på cafe

7a hej; b goddag/godformiddag; c farvel; d godnat; e må jeg bede om/kan jeg få en kaffe?; f kan jeg få regningen

UNIT 4
Money
Cash machine

Vocabulary builder
Red, green, blue, orange, jacket, rain, snow

Conversation 1

1 Lise buys a dress, Lotte buys a scarf.

2a She is going to a party; **b** The first one is too small; **c** Size 40; **d** Red

3 There are three versions: rød/rødt/røde.

Language discovery
vil = a desire, skal = a command

Practice

1

Basic form	't' form	'e' form
hvid	hvidt	hvide
ny	nyt	nye
høj	højt	høje
gammel	gammelt	gamle
kold	koldt	kolde
stor	stort	store
ung	unge	unge
smuk	smukt	smukke
glad	gladt	glade

2a sort; **b** brune; **c** blå; **d** lyserød; **e** grønne
3a Jeg vil gerne have en rød kjole i størrelse 42; **b** Jeg vil gerne have en blå skjorte i størrelse 38
4a kan; **b** må; **c** vil; **d** skal; **e** må; **f** bør

Conversation 2
1 The sun is shining
2 sol
3 A scarf;
4 400 kr

Reading
a vejrudsigt; **b** Bornholm; **c** Wind; **d** Det er dejligt vejr; **e** Det er dårligt vejr

Speaking

Karl	Ja, det er dårligt vejr!
Karl	Imorgen skinner solen
Karl	Fra vejrudsigten.

Test yourself
1a skoene er sorte; **b** huset er rødt; **c** jeg har et blåt tørklæde; **d** børnene har fem grønne æbler
2a kan; **b** må; **c** skal; **d** vil
3 For example, idag skinner solen/idag regner det/idag er det regnvejr/ idag blæser det
4a Jeg vil gerne have en hvis skjorte; **b** Jeg vil gerne have en nederdel i størrelse 40; **c** Kan jeg betale med kort

UNIT 5
Transport in Denmark
Seat reservation

Vocabulary builder
Timetable, window seat

Conversation 1
1 Sunday midday
2a The 10.45 is a direct train; **b** Talk; **c** Five past ten
3 min, din/jeres, vores
4 past = over; to = i

Language discovery
Telling time: Halv ti

Practice
1b mine; **c** vores; **d** deres; **e** dit; **f** jeres; **g** dets; **h** hans
2a sit; **b** hans; **c** sine; **d** sin; **e** hendes; **f** hans
3a tyve minutter over tre; **b** ti minutter i et; **c** fem minutter i elleve; **d** kvart over tolv; **e** fem minutter over halv tolv; **f** halv tolv; **g** kvart over ti; **h** kvart i syv; **i** fem minutter over halv fire

Conversation 2
1 Østergade, he can get a 14 or a 26
2a Round the corner; **b** Yes (de går tit)

Reading
a 07.29 from Nørregade; **b** No, that bus is only on schooldays; **c** 16.14 from Nørregade

Writing
An example could be: Hej. Jeg tager bussen fra Nørregade 18.14, ankommer Kirkegade 18.40. Vi ses.

Speaking
Ida	Jeg vil gerne have en retur billet til Nyborg
Ida	Ja, tak
Ida	Elleve femogfyrre
Ida	Imorgen klokken tretten nul fem
Ida	Tak

Test yourself
1a mit; **b** hans; **c** din; **d** vores; **e** sine; **f** deres
2a kvart over to; **b** klokken otte; **c** halv seks; **d** ti minutter over fire; **e** fem minutter i halv elleve
3a Jeg vil gerne have en returbillet til Roskilde; **b** Jeg vil gerne have en pladsbillet i en stillekupe; **c** Hvor afgår toget til Nyborg fra?

UNIT 6
Compound words
Three words (cykel-hjelm-kampagne), bike helmet campaign

Vocabulary builder
Roundabout, after

Conversation 1
1 To get bus number 44
2 No, it is not far, 10–15 minutes on foot
3 The verbs are: gå, tag, drej, bliv, there is no 'e' at the end
4 femte
5 nede ved togstationen

Language discovery, adverbs of place
The **e** is dropped and it becomes ned

Practice
1a drej; **b** køb; **c** snak; **d** gå; **e** spis; **f** kør
2a oppe; **b** ud; **c** inde; **d** hjemme
3a tredje; **b** femte; **c** enogtyvende; **d** syvende; **e** fjortende
4a 21.9; **b** 31.7; **c** 16.4; **d** 6.1; **e** 11.11; **f** 29.3

Reading
1 a 2; **b** 5; **c** 3; **d** 1; **e** 6; **f** 8; **g** 12; **h** 11; **i** 9; **j** 4; **k** 10; **l** 7
2 a 1; **b** 9; **c** 6; **d** 2; **e** 5; **f** 8; **g** 10; **h** 3; **i** 11; **j** 4; **k** 12; **l** 7

Conversation 2
1 Three nights
2 Third floor
3 In the lift

Speaking

Sten	Jeg kan den treogtyvende eller den femogtyvende april.
Sten	Ved Hotel Danica. Vi kan spise frokost der.
Sten	Halv et.
Sten	Vi ses den treogtyvende.

Test yourself

1a Undskyld, kan du fortælle mig hvor Hotel Scandinavia er? **b** Undskyld, hvordan kommer jeg fra lufthavnen til Valby? **c** Undskyld, hvor er restauranten?

2a drej; **b** kør; **c** gå

3a Hvor skal du hen?; **b** jeg går op til Hanne; **c** bussen holder need ved stationen; **d** kom ind!

4 For example, 17.09.71

5 For example, syttende september

REVIEW 2

1a grønne; **b** højt; **c** glad/nye; **d** sort/gult; **e** gammel

2 6.30, 9.15, 12.10, 8.35, 4.45, 7.25, 11.50

3a kan; **b** må; **c** vil; **d** skal

4a Rain and wind; **b** Autumn; **c** On Sealand (Sjælland)

5a Jeg har dine/jeres billetter i min lomme. **b** Vores børn hedder Peter og Louise. **c** Der er Sophie, det er hendes kjole. **d** Han elsker sin kone. **e** Det er deres hus.

6a Turn left; **b** third exit; **c** to the right

7a Drej til venstre i krydset; **b** Drik vand hver dag; **c** Sæt dig på stolen; **d** Skriv dit navn her

8a 21.; **b** 13.; **c** 8.; **d** 31.; **e** 14.; **f** 4.

UNIT 7
Politics

'Borgen' is short for Christiansborg (en borg means a castle).

Vocabulary builder

Maths, history, physics/chemistry nature/technology studies

Conversation 1

1 Five subjects (dansk, idræt, engelsk, matematik, billedkunst)

2 læste, læse, har læst

3 Jeg kan godt lide …

4 Jeg vil hellere …

Practice

1

Infinitiv	Nutid	Datid	Førnutid	Førdatid
at snakke	snakker	snakkede	har snakket	havde snakket
at købe	køber	købte	har købt	havde købt
at arbejde	arbejder	arbejdede	har arbejdet	havde arbejdet
at være	er	var	har været	havde været
at spise	spiser	spiste	har spist	havde spist
at bo	bor	boede	har boet	havde boet
at have	har	havde	har haft	havde haft

2a cyklede; **b** har arbejdet; **c** snakkede; **d** besøgte; **e** har været (assuming they are still friends); **f** har rejst

3a Jeg kan ikke lide laks /jeg bryder mig ikke om laks; **b** Jeg foretrækker danske film; **c** Jeg kan godt lide at gå; **d** Jeg vil hellere gå end køre.

Conversation 2

1 Eight (Enhedslisten, Socialistisk Folkeparti, Socialdemokratiet, de konservative, Venstre, Dansk Folkeparti, Liberal Alliance, Det Radikale Venstre)
2 The name of the original groupings in parliament were højre and venstre
3 In the middle

Reading

a Signe Jensen won a prize for her book; **b** No, she lived in Germany for two years; **c** at læse; **d** Six

Writing

The entry could be something like this:
Jeg blev født i Slagelse i 1984, men i 1990 flyttede vi til Korsør. Fra 2002 til 2007 læste jeg matematik ved Aarhus Universitet, før jeg blev lærer i Herfølge. Jeg har været medlem af Folketinget siden 2014 og jeg bor i Herfølge med min kone og vores to børn.

Test yourself

1a Johan talte med Birgitte igår; **b** Han har læst engelsk i fire år; **c** I sidste måned læste jeg tre bøger; **d** Vi har boet i Danmark siden 2010.
2a har arbejdet; b boede; c købte; d har læst; e drak; f har rejst
3a Jeg elsker tomater; **b** Jeg foretrækker ris fremfor pasta; **c** Jeg kan ikke lide øl/Jeg bryder mig ikke om øl.

UNIT 8
Dansk frokost
pølse, brød

Vocabulary builder
knife

Conversation 1
1 leverpostej, rugbrød, spegepølse, remoulade, rullepølse
2 Thanks, but no thanks
3 skål
4 hurtig, sund, they have different endings

Practice
1a John er ældre end Carl; **b** Sarah er hurtigst, men Anna er mest
intelligent; **c** Vand er sundere end vin; **d** En bil er hurtig, men et tog er
hurtigere; **e** Peter er mindre end Hans, men Leo er mindst
2a steges; **b** males; **c** stjæles/bliver stjålet; **d** piskes; **e** spises/bliver spist
3 a 4; **b** 5 or 1; **c** 2; **d** 1 or 5; **e** 3

Conversation 2
1 hjemmelavet dildsnaps; **2** Det var en hyggelig eftermiddag; **3** Vi fik nok
at spise.

Reading
a Pudding rice, milk, cream, almonds; **b** Cold; **c** Warm cherry sauce;
d Passive form (bringes) and imperative (bland).

Writing
An example could be: Kære Louise. Tak for sidst. Det var en hyggelig aften
og maden var super. Kærlig hilsen Lene.

Speaking

Tove	Må jeg bede om smørret?
Tove	Vil du også række mig spegepølsen?
Tove	Tak skal du have. Det smager dejligt.
Tove	Skål!

Test yourself

1

stor	større	størst
sød	sødere	sødest
nem	nemmere	nemmest
lille	mindre	mindst
dejlig	dejligere	dejligst

2a Mange cykler bliver stjålet/stjæles hver dag; **b** Kagen serveres med flødeskum; **c** Maden spises af hunden/Maden bliver spist af hunden.
3a Tak for mad; **b** Tak for sidst; **c** Tak for lån.
4a Må jeg bede om sukkeret; **b** Vil du række mig smørret

UNIT 9
Sport in Denmark
DM: Danmarks Mesterskaberne/Danish Championships; VM: Verdens Mesterskaberne/World Championships

Vocabulary builder
To win, to score, stadium, to ride

Conversation 1
1 Going to the cinema, going to the swimming pool, going to an international football match, going to a concert in Tivoli
2 She doesn't like films by Susanne Bier
3 She finds it boring
4 synes, tror
5 more os, hygge os

Practice
1a som; **b** der; **c** der; **d** som; **e** der
2a sig; **b** mig; **c** sig; **d** dig; **e** os; **f** sig
3a Jeg synes det er en god ide; **b** Jeg tror der er en concert imorgen; **c** Hvad synes du?/Hvad mener du?; **d** Jeg er overbevist om at solen skinner imorgen.

Reading
a Three (FC Midtjylland v FC København, OB v Aab, Brøndby v Esbjerg); **b** It was a draw between FC Midtjylland and FC København, OB won over Aab and Brøndby won over Esbjerg; **c** udligne; **d** They had a player sent off.

Conversation 2
1 No, she has gone for a walk
2 Kan jeg give en besked
3 Jeg giver beskeden videre
4 Er der andet

Speaking
Erik	Ja, hvad er det?
Erik	Simon kommer klokken 3. Er der andet?
Erik	Ha ha, tak. Vi ses

Writing
For example: Hej Sophie. Cristian henter dig kl. 19.30. I skal i biografen. Husk hans tørklæde.

Test yourself
1a Han barberer sig hver morgen; **b** Vi keder os; **c** Sæt dig ned!; **d** Jeg morer mig; **e** De skyndte sig i skole
2a som/der; **b** som; **c** som/der; **d** som/der; **e** som
3a Jeg synes det er en god ide; **b** Jeg synes jakken er meget dyr; **c** Jeg tror vi skal dreje til højre; **d** Jeg mener/tror han er 20 år.

UNIT 10
Holidays
Advent calendar, Christmas lunch, Santa Claus

Vocabulary builder
Confirmation, silver anniversary, golden anniversay

Conversation 1
1 Wine, candle sticks, a vase, coffee jug
2 nogle, noget, nogen
3 this, those

Practice
1a Den her/Denne sofa er rød; **b** Det der/Det træ er meget højt; **c** De her/Disse katte er hvide, men de der er sorte; **d** Den her/Denne bog er lang
2a Jeg sender et postkort til dig; **b** Lene drikker ikke mælk; **c** Har du en saks?; **d** Vil du have rødvin?; **e** Husk at drikke vand; **f** Jeg har en kusine, der bor på Samsø.
3a noget; **b** nogle; **c** nogen; **d** nogen; **e** noget; **f** nogen

Listening
a Tivoli will be open on the day of Christmas Eve for the first time;
b Tourists, people who don't celebrate traditional Christmas and families with children; **c** They hope it will become a permanent tradition.

Reading
a Yes, she had a lovely day; **b** A watch, jewellery, iPad and 10,000 kr; **c** Her aunt Susan and her uncle Nikolaj

Writing
For example: Kære Signe og Martin. Tak for invitationen til jeres bryllup. Vi vil gerne komme og glæder os til dagen. Kærlig hilsen X

Speaking
Kære Jesper. Idag er en god dag. Det er idag vi fejrer en mand som er meget sjov, meget klog og en meget god ven. Jeg vil gerne sige tillykke med fødselsdagen og jeg glæder mig til mange flere år med dig. Tillykke med fødselsdagen og skål!

Test yourself
1a Den her/Denne; **b** De her/disse, de der/disse; **c** Det her/Dette; **d** Den her/Denne
2 Countable: saks, oplysning, kjole, avis. Uncountable: mælk, penge, smørrebrød, musik, tøj
3a Vil du have noget te?; **b** Jeg har ikke nogen æbler; **c** Vil du købe nogle kager?; **d** Hun har ikke nogen penge; **e** Kan du hjælpe mig med noget?

REVIEW 3
1a Jeg boede i Odense i 5 år; **b** John læste en bog igår; **c** Jeg har boet i Danmark i 7 år; **d** De har købt et stort hus; **e** Hun har været læge i 15 år; **f** De dansede hele natten; **g** Vi har cyklet 50 km nu.
2

Adjective	Comparative	Superlative
stor	større	størst
glad	gladere	gladest
nem	nemmere	nemmest
lille	mindre	mindst
gammel	ældre	ældst
hurtig	hurtigere	hurtigst
interessant	mere interessant	mest interessant

3a serveres/bliver serveret; **b** stjæles/bliver ofte stjålet; **c** spises/bliver spist;
d hejses/bliver flaget hejst
4a sig/sig; **b** os; **c** mig; **d** sig; **e** dig
5 a 4; **b** 5; **c** 1; **d** 3; **e** 2
6a nogen; **b** noget; **c** nogle; **d** noget
7a Tak for hjælpen; **b** Tak for mad; **c** Tak for idag.
8a Jane wants a small party for the family but Niels wants a big party.
b Jane is not keen on big parties. **c** Their children, grandchildren, friends,
neighbours and colleagues. **d** Niels is phoning to enquire about prices,
Jane is making a guest list.

Danish–English glossary

afgang	*departure*
aften (-en, -er)	*evening*
allerede	*already*
alletiders	*great*
ankomst	*arrival*
appelsin (-en, -er)	*orange*
arbejde (arbejdede, arbejdet)	*work*
avis (-en, -er)	*newspaper*
bagefter	*afterwards*
barn (-et, børn)	*child*
bede (bad, bedt)	*ask, pray*
besked (-en, -er)	*message*
besøge (besøgte, besøgt)	*visit*
bestille (bestilte, bestilt)	*book/order*
bil (-en, -er)	*car*
billede (-t, -r)	*picture*
billet (-en, -er)	*ticket*
billig	*cheap*
biograf (-en, -er)	*cinema*
blæst (-en)	*wind*
blå	*blue*
bo (boede, boet)	*live*
bog (-en, bøger)	*book*
bold (-en, -e)	*ball*
bord (-et, -e)	*table*
bror (-en, brødre)	*brother*
brun	*brown*
bryllup (-pet, -per)	*wedding*
brød (-et, -)	*bread*
bukser (-ne)	*trousers*
bus (-sen, -ser)	*bus*
busstoppested (-et, -er)	*bus stop*
bør (burde, burdet)	*should*
cykel (cyklen, cykler)	*bicycle*
cykelhjelm (-en, -e)	*bike helmet*
cykelsti (-en, -er)	*cycle path*
cykle (cyklede, cyklet)	*cycle*
dag (-en, -e)	*day*

dato (-en, -er)	*date*
dejlig	*lovely*
dele (delte, delt)	*share*
derovre	*over there*
desværre	*unfortunately*
direkte	*direct*
dommer (-en, -e)	*referee/judge*
dreje (drejede, drejet)	*turn*
dreng (-en, -e)	*boy*
drikke (drak, drukket)	*drink*
drikkepenge	*tip*
dyr	*expensive*
dyr (-et, -)	*animal*
dør (-en, -e)	*door*
efter	*after*
efterår (-et, -)	*autumn*
elske (elskede, elsket)	*love*
ensrettet	*one way*
etage (-n, -r)	*floor*
familie (-n, -r)	*family*
far (-en, fædre)	*father/dad*
farlig	*dangerous*
farvel	*goodbye*
fejre (fejrede, fejret)	*celebrate*
ferie (-n, -r)	*holiday*
film (-en, -)	*film*
finde (fandt, fundet)	*find*
flaske (-n, -r)	*bottle*
flere	*more*
flot	*nice/handsome*
fløde (-n)	*cream*
flødeskum (-met)	*whipped cream*
fodbold	*football*
forældre (-ne)	*parents*
forår (-et, -)	*spring*
forbudt	*forbidden*
frakørsel (-en, -er)	*exit*
frikadelle (-n, -r)	*meatballs*
frikvarter (-et, -)	*break (at school)*
frimærke (-t, -r)	*stamp*
frokost (-en, -er)	*lunch*
fætter (-en, fætre)	*cousin (male)*
fødselsdag (-en, -e)	*birthday*

før	before
gade (-n, -r)	street
gaffel (gaflen, gafler)	fork
gammel	old
gave (-n, -r)	present
gide (gad, gidet)	be bothered
gift med	married to
glad	happy
glas (-set, -)	glass
glat	slippery
god (bedre, bedst)	good
goddag	hello
grøn	green
grå	grey
gul	yellow
gulerod (-en, -rødder)	carrot
gæst (-en, -er)	guest
gå (gik, gået)	go/walk
halstørklæde	scarf (for winter)
have (havde, haft)	have
have travlt	be busy
hedde (hed, heddet)	be called
hej	hi
hejse (hejste, hejst)	raise
hellere	rather
hente (hentede, hentet)	pick up
herfra	from here
historie (-n, -r)	story
hjem	home
hjælpe (hjalp, hjulpet)	help
hund (-en, -e)	dog
hundrede (-r)	hundred
hus (-et, -e)	house
hvid	white
hyggelig	nice, cosy
høj	tall
højre	right (opposite of left)
håndbold	handball
i stedet for	instead
imorgen	tomorrow
ind	in
ingen	nobody/none
ingeniør (-en, -e)	engineer

instruktør (-en, -e)	*film/theatre director*
jordbær (-ret, -)	*strawberry*
jul	*Christmas*
juleaften	*Christmas Eve*
julegave (-n, -r)	*Christmas present*
julekalender (-en, -e)	*advent calendar*
julemand	*Santa Claus*
kaffe (-n)	*coffee*
kage (-n, -r)	*cake*
kamp (-en, -e)	*match/fight*
kan (kunne, kunnet)	*can*
kande (-n, -r)	*jug*
kartoffel (-en, -er)	*potato*
kasse (-n, -r)	*box*
kat (-ten, -te)	*cat*
kende (kendte, kendt)	*know*
kirsebær (-ret, -)	*cherry*
kjole (-n, -r)	*dress*
klasse (-n, -r)	*school year/grade*
kniv (-en, -e)	*knife*
komme (kom, kommet)	*come*
kone (-n, -r)	*wife*
kontanter (-ne)	*cash*
kop (-pen, -per)	*cup*
kryds (-et, -)	*junction*
kuffert (-en, -er)	*suitcase*
kun	*only*
kusine (-n, -r)	*cousin (female)*
kylling (-en, -er)	*chicken*
kære	*dear*
kæreste (-n, -r)	*boyfriend/girlfriend*
kø (-en, -er)	*queue*
købe (købte, købt)	*buy*
kød (-et)	*meat*
køreplan (-en, -er)	*timetable*
laks (-en, -)	*salmon*
låne (lånte, lånt)	*borrow*
lave (lavede, lavet)	*do*
lege (legede, leget)	*play*
legetøj (-et)	*toys*
leverpostej (-en, -er)	*liver paté*
ligeud	*straight ahead*
lilla	*purple*
lyd (-en, -e)	*sound*

lyn (-et, -)	*lightning*
lyserød	*pink*
lysestage (-n, -r)	*candlestick*
læge (-n, -r)	*doctor*
lære (lærte, lært)	*learn/teach*
lærer (-en, -e)	*teacher*
læse (læste, læst)	*read*
løn (-nen)	*wages*
mad (-en)	*food*
male (malede, malet)	*paint*
mand (-en, mænd)	*man/husband*
mandel (mandlen, mandler)	*almond*
mange	*a lot/many*
mene (mente, ment)	*think (opinion)*
menukort (-et, -)	*menu*
middagstid	*lunchtime*
mobil (-en, -er)	*mobile phone*
mor (-en, mødre)	*mother/mum*
morgen (-en, er)	*morning*
motionscenter (-et, -re)	*gym*
mund (-en, -e)	*mouth*
musik (-ken)	*music*
mælk (-en)	*milk*
mæt	*full up*
møde (mødte, mødt)	*meet*
mønt (-en, -er)	*coin*
må (måtte, måttet)	*may/have to*
måned (-en, -er)	*month*
nabo (-en, -er)	*neighbour*
nat (-ten, nætter)	*night*
naturligvis	*naturally*
navn (-et, -e)	*name*
nem	*easy*
nok	*probably/enough*
nytår	*New Year*
næste	*next*
nøgle (-n, -r)	*key*
når	*when*
og	*and*
også	*too*
område (-t, -r)	*area*
op	*up*
oplysning (-en, -er)	*information*
orange	*orange (colour)*

ordbog (-en, -bøger)	*dictionary*
ofte	*often*
ost (-en, -e)	*cheese*
parti (-et, -er)	*political party*
passe (passede, passet)	*fit/look after*
penge (-ne)	*money*
pengeautomat (-en, -er)	*cash machine*
person (-en, -er)	*person*
pige (-n, -r)	*girl*
pladsbillet (-ten, -ter)	*seat reservation*
postkort (-et, -)	*postcard*
problem (-et, -er)	*problem*
prøve (prøvede, prøvet)	*try*
pølse (-n, -r)	*sausage*
påske	*Easter*
regn (-en)	*rain*
regning (-en, -er)	*bill*
reje (-n, -r)	*prawn*
rejse (-n, -r)	*journey*
rejse (rejste, rejst)	*travel*
resultat (-et, -er)	*result*
rigtig	*really/right (correct)*
rundkørsel (-en, -er)	*roundabout*
rød	*red*
saks (-en, -e)	*scissors*
score (scorede, scoret)	*score*
selvfølgelig	*of course*
sende (sendte, sendt)	*send*
senere	*later*
sidde (sad, siddet)	*sit*
sidste	*last*
sikre (sikrede, sikret)	*secure*
sild (-en, -)	*herring*
sjov	*funny*
skal	*have to (future tense)*
ske (-en, -er)	*spoon*
skinke (-n, -r)	*ham*
sko (-en, -)	*shoes*
skole (-n, -r)	*school*
skære (skar, skåret)	*cut*
skål!	*cheers!*
slips (-et, -)	*tie*
slud	*sleet*
slå (slog, slået)	*hit*

smage (smagte, smagt)	*taste*
smuk	*beautiful*
smør (-ret)	*butter*
smørrebrød (-et)	*open sandwiches*
snakke (snakkede, snakket)	*talk*
sne (-en)	*snow*
sodavand (-en, -)	*fizzy drink*
sokker	*socks*
sol (-en, -e)	*sun*
solskin (-net)	*sunshine*
sommer (-en, somre)	*summer*
sort	*black*
sove (sov, sovet)	*sleep*
spille (spillede, spillet)	*play*
spiller (-en, -e)	*player*
sprog (-et, -)	*language*
stadig	*still*
stearinlys (-et, -)	*candle*
sted (-et, -er)	*place*
stege (stegte, stegt)	*fry*
stol (-en, -e)	*chair*
stor	*big*
størrelse (-n, -r)	*size*
sukker (-et)	*sugar*
sulten	*hungry*
sund	*healthy*
svømmehal (-len, -ler)	*swimming pool*
sætte (satte, sat)	*put/set*
sød	*sweet*
søskende	*siblings*
søster (-en, søstre)	*sister*
tabe (tabte, tabt)	*lose*
tage (tog, taget)	*take*
tak	*thank you*
tale (talte, talt)	*speak*
tallerken (-en, -er)	*plate*
teater (-teatret, teatre)	*theatre*
tid (-en)	*time*
tidspunkt (-et, -er)	*time (specific)*
tillykke	*congratulations*
time (-n, -r)	*lesson*
time (-n, -r)	*hour*
tit	*often*
tjener (-en, -e)	*waiter*

tog (-et, -)	train
togstation (-en, -er)	train station
torden (-en)	thunder
trafiklys (-et, -)	traffic light
trafikprop (-pen, -per)	traffic jam
trappe (-n, -r)	staircase
tro (troede, troet)	believe
træ (-et, -er)	tree
tung	heavy
tusind	thousand
tænde (tændte, tændt)	switch on
tøj (-et)	clothes
tørklæde (-t, -r)	scarf
ud	out
udligne (udlignede, udlignet)	equalize
udvide (udvidede, udvidet)	extend/expand
uge (-n, -r)	week
undervise (underviste, undervist)	teach
undskyld	excuse me/sorry
ung	young
vase (-n, -r)	vase
vaske (vaskede, vasket)	wash
vej (-en, -e)	road
vejarbejde (-t)	roadworks
vejr (-et)	weather
vejrudsigt (-en, -er)	weather forecast
ven (-nen, -ner)	friend
veninde (-n, -r)	female friend
venstre	left
vente (ventede, ventet)	wait
vi ses	see you later
vil (ville, villet)	want
vild	wild/crazy
vinde (vandt, vundet)	win
vinter (-en, vintre)	winter
vise (viste, vist)	show
værelse (-t, -r)	room
værsgo	here you go
æble (-t, -r)	apple
øje (-t, øjne)	eye
øl (-len, -)	beer
øre (-t, -r)	ear
år (-et, -)	year

English–Danish glossary

advent calendar	julekalender (-en, -e)
after	efter
afterwards	bagefter
almond	mandel (mandlen, mandler)
already	allerede
and	og
animal	dyr (-et, -)
apple	æble (-t, -r)
area	område (-t, -r)
arrival	ankomst
ask/pray	bede (bad, bedt)
autumn	efterår (-et, -)
ball	bold (-en, -e)
be bothered	gide (gad, gidet)
be busy	have travlt
be called	hedde (hed, heddet)
beautiful	smuk
beer	øl (-len, -)
before	før
believe	tro (troede, troet)
bicycle	cykel (cyklen, cykler)
big	stor (større, størst)
bike helmet	cykelhjelm (-en, -e)
bill	regning (-n, -r)
birthday	fødselsdag (-en, -e)
black	sort
blue	blå
book	bog (-en, bøger)
book/order	bestille (bestilte, bestilt)
borrow	låne (lånte, lånt)
bottle	flaske (-n, -r)
box	kasse (-n, -r)
boy	dreng (-en, -e)
boyfriend/girlfriend	kæreste (-n, -r)
bread	brød (-et, -)
break (at school)	frikvarter (-et, -)
brother	bror (-en, brødre)
brown	brun
bus	bus (-sen, ser)

bus stop	busstoppested (-et, -er)
butter	smør (-ret)
buy	købe (købte, købt)
cake	kage (-n, -r)
can	kan (kunne, kunnet)
candle	stearinlys (-et, -)
candlestick	lysestage (-n, -r)
car	bil (-en, -er)
carrot	gulerod (-en, -rødder)
cash	kontanter (-ne)
cash machine	pengeautomat (-en, -er)
cat	kat (-ten, -te)
celebrate	fejre (fejrede, fejret)
chair	stol (-en, -e)
cheap	billig
cheers!	skål!
cheese	ost (-en, -e)
cherry	kirsebær (-ret, -)
chicken	kylling (-en, -er)
child	barn (-et, børn)
Christmas	jul
Christmas Eve	juleaften
Christmas present	julegave (-n, -r)
cinema	biograf (-en, -er)
clothes	tøj (-et)
coffee	kaffe (-n)
coin	mønt (-en, -er)
come	komme (kom, kommet)
congratulations	tillykke
cousin (female)	kusine (-n, -r)
cousin (male)	fætter (-en, fætre)
cream	fløde (-n)
cup	kop (-pen, -per)
cut	skære (skar, skåret)
cycle	cykle (cyklede, cyklet)
cycle path	cykelsti (-en, -er)
dangerous	farlig
date	dato (-en, -er)
day	dag (-en, -e)
dear	kære
departure	afgang
dictionary	ordbog (-en, -bøger)
direct	direkte
director	instruktør (-en, -e)

do	lave (lavede, lavet)
doctor	læge (-n, -r)
dog	hund (-en, -e)
door	dør (-en, -e)
dress	kjole (-n, -r)
drink	drikke (drak, drukket)
ear	øre (-t, -r)
Easter	påske
easy	nem
engineer	ingeniør (-en, -e)
equalize	udligne (udlignede, udlignet)
evening	aften (-en, -er)
excuse me/sorry	undskyld
exit	frakørsel (-en, -er)
expensive	dyr
extend/expand	udvide (udvidede, udvidet)
eye	øje (-t, øjne)
family	familie (-n, -r)
father/dad	far (-en, fædre)
film	film (-en, -)
find	finde (fandt, fundet)
fit	passe (passede, passet)
fizzy drink	sodavand (-en, -)
floor	etage (-n, -r)
food	mad (-en)
football	fodbold
forbidden	forbudt
fork	gaffel (gaflen, gafler)
friend	ven (-nen, -ner)
friend (female)	veninde (-n, -r)
from here	herfra
fry	stege (stegte, stegt)
full up	mæt
funny	sjov
girl	pige (-n, -r)
girlfriend/boyfriend	kæreste (-n, -r)
glass	glas (-set, -)
go	gå (gik, gået)
good	god (bedre, bedst)
goodbye	farvel
great	alletiders
green	grøn
grey	grå
guest	gæst (-en, -er)

gym	motionscenter (-et, re)
ham	skinke (-n, -r)
handball	håndbold
happy	glad
have	have (havde, haft)
have to	skal (skulle, skullet)
healthy	sund
heavy	tung
hello	goddag
help	hjælpe (hjalp, hjulpet)
here you are	værsgo
herring	sild (-en, -)
hi	hej
hit	slå (slog, slået)
holiday	ferie (-n, -r)
home	hjem
hour	time (-n, -r)
house	hus (-et, -e)
hundred	hundrede (-r)
hungry	sulten
husband	mand (-en, mænd)
in	ind
information	oplysning (-en, -er)
instead	i stedet for
journey	rejse (-n, -r)
jug	kande (-n, -r)
junction	kryds (-et, -)
key	nøgle (-n, -r)
knife	kniv (-en, -e)
know	kende (kendte, kendt)
language	sprog (-et, -)
last	sidste
later	senere
learn	lære (lærte, lært)
left	venstre
lesson	time (-n, -r)
lightening	lyn (-et, -o)
live	bo (boede, boet)
liver paté	leverpostej (-en, -er)
lose	tabe (tabte, tabt)
love	elske (elskede, elsket)
lovely	dejlig
lunch	frokost (-en, -er)
lunchtime	middagstid

man	mand (-en, mænd)
many	mange
married to	gift med
match	kamp (-en, -e)
may	må (måtte, måttet)
meat	kød (-et)
meatballs	frikadelle (-n, -r)
meet	møde (mødte, mødt)
menu	menukort (-et, -)
message	besked (-en, -er)
milk	mælk (-en)
mobile phone	mobil (-en, -er)
money	penge (-ne)
month	måned (-en, -er)
more	flere
morning	morgen (-en, er)
mother/mum	mor (-en, mødre)
mouth	mund (-en, -e)
music	musik (-ken)
name	navn (-et, -e)
naturally	naturligvis
neighbour	nabo (-en, -er)
New Year	nytår
newspaper	avis (-en, -er)
next	næste
nice/cosy	hyggelig
nice (looking)	flot
night	nat (-ten, nætter)
nobody/none	ingen
of course	selvfølgelig
often	ofte
often	tit
old	gammel (ældre, ældst)
one-way	ensrettet
only	kun
open sandwiches	smørrebrød (-et)
orange (fruit)	appelsin (-en, er)
orange (colour)	orange
out	ud
over there	derovre
paint	male (malede, malet)
parents	forældre (-ne)
person	person (-en, -er)
pick up	hente (hentede, hentet)

picture	billede (-et, -er)
pink	lyserød
place	sted (-t, -r)
plate	tallerken (-en, -er)
play	lege (legede, leget)/spille (spillede, spillet)
player	spiller (-en, -e)
political party	parti (-et, -er)
postcard	postkort (-et, -)
potato	kartoffel (-en, -er)
prawn	reje (-n, -r)
present	gave (-n, -r)
probably	nok
problem	problem (-et, -er)
purple	lilla
question	spørgsmål
queue	kø (-en, -er)
rain	regn (-en)
raise	hejse (hejste, hejst)
rather	hellere
read	læse (læste, læst)
really	rigtig
red	rød
referee	dommer (-en, -e)
result	resultat (-et, -er)
right	højre
right (correct)	rigtigt
road	vej (-en, -e)
road works	vejarbejde (-t)
room	værelse (-t, -r)
roundabout	rundkørsel (-en, -er)
salmon	laks (-en, -)
Santa Claus	julemand (-en)
sausage	pølse (-n, -r)
scarf	tørklæde (-t, -r)
scarf (for winter)	halstørklæde
school	skole (-n, -r)
school year/grade	klasse (-n, -r)
scissors	saks (-en, -e)
score	score (scorede, scoret)
seat reservation	pladsbillet (-ten, -ter)
secure	sikre (sikrede, sikret)
see you later	vi ses
send	sende (sendte, sendt)

share	dele (delte, delt)
should	burde (bør, burde, burdet)
show	vise (viste, vist)
siblings	søskende
sister	søster (-en, søstre)
sit	sidde (sad, siddet)
size	størrelse (-n, -r)
sleep	sove (sov, sovet)
sleet	slud
slippery	glat
snow	sne (-en)
socks	sokker
sound	lyd (-en, -e)
speak	tale (talte, talt)
spoon	ske (-en, -er)
spring	forår (-et, -)
staircase	trappe (-n, -r)
stamp	frimærke (-t, -r)
still	stadig
story	historie (-n, -r)
straight ahead	ligeud
strawberry	jordbær (-ret, -)
street	gade (-n, -r)
sugar	sukker (-et)
suitcase	kuffert (-en, -er)
summer	sommer (-en, somre)
sun	sol (-en, -e)
sunshine	solskin (-net)
sweet	sød
swimming pool	svømmehal (-len, -ler)
switch on	tænde (tændte, tændt)
table	bord (-et, -e)
take	tage (tog, taget)
talk	snakke (snakkede, snakket)
tall	høj
taste	smage (smagte, smagt)
teach	undervise (underviste, undervist)
teacher	lærer (-en, -e)
thank you	tak
theatre	teater (teatret, teatre)
think (opinion)	mene (mente, ment)
thousand	tusind (-e)
thunder	torden (-en)

ticket	billet (-en, -er)
tie	slips (-et, -)
time	tid (-en)
time (specific)	tidspunkt (-et, -er)
timetable	køreplan (-en, -er)
tip	drikkepenge
tomorrow	imorgen
too	også
toys	legetøj (-et)
traffic light	trafiklys (-et, -)
traffic jam	trafikprop (-pen, -per)
train	tog (-et, -)
train station	togstation (-en, -er)
travel	rejse (rejste, rejst)
tree	træ (-et, -er)
trousers	bukser
try	prøve (prøvede, prøvet)
turn	dreje (drejede, drejet)
unfortunately	desværre
up	op
vase	vase (-n, -r)
visit	besøge (besøgte, besøgt)
wages	løn (-nen)
wait	vente (ventede, ventet)
waiter	tjener (-en, -e)
walk	gå (gik, gået)
want	vil (ville, villet)
wash	vaske (vaskede, vasket)
weather	vejr (-et)
weather forecast	vejrudsigt (-en, -er)
wedding	bryllup (-et, -er)
week	uge (-n, -r)
when	når
whipped cream	flødeskum (-met)
white	hvid
wife	kone (-n, -r)
wild	vild
win	vinde (vandt, vundet)
wind	blæst (-en)
winter	vinter (-en, vintre)
work	arbejde (arbejde, arbejdet)
year	år (-et, -)
yellow	gul
young	ung (yngre, yngst)

"Global scale" of the Common European Framework of Reference for Languages: learning, teaching, assessment (CEFR)

Advanced	CEFR LEVEL C2	Can understand with ease virtually everything heard or read. Can summarise information from different spoken and written sources, reconstructing arguments and accounts in a coherent presentation. Can express him/herself spontaneously, very fluently and precisely, differentiating finer shades of meaning even in more complex situations.
Advanced	CEFR LEVEL C1	Can understand a wide range of demanding, longer texts, and recognise implicit meaning. Can express him/herself fluently and spontaneously without much obvious searching for expressions. Can use language flexibly and effectively for social, academic and professional purposes. Can produce clear, well-structured, detailed text on complex subjects, showing controlled use of organisational patterns, connectors and cohesive devices.
Intermediate	CEFR LEVEL B2 (A Level)	Can understand the main ideas of complex text on both concrete and abstract topics, including technical discussions in his/her field of specialisation. Can interact with a degree of fluency and spontaneity that makes regular interaction with native speakers quite possible without strain for either party. Can produce clear, detailed text on a wide range of subjects and explain a viewpoint on a topical issue giving the advantages and disadvantages of various options.
Intermediate	CEFR LEVEL B1 (Higher GCSE)	Can understand the main points of clear standard input on familiar matters regularly encountered in work, school, leisure, etc. Can deal with most situations likely to arise whilst travelling in an area where the language is spoken. Can produce simple connected text on topics which are familiar or of personal interest. Can describe experiences and events, dreams, hopes and ambitions and briefly give reasons and explanations for opinions and plans.
Beginner	CEFR LEVEL A2: (Foundation GCSE)	Can understand sentences and frequently used expressions related to areas of most immediate relevance (e.g. very basic personal and family information, shopping, local geography, employment). Can communicate in simple and routine tasks requiring a simple and direct exchange of information on familiar and routine matters. Can describe in simple terms aspects of his/her background, immediate environment and matters in areas of immediate need.
Beginner	CEFR LEVEL A1	Can understand and use familiar everyday expressions and very basic phrases aimed at the satisfaction of needs of a concrete type. Can introduce him/herself and others and can ask and answer questions about personal details such as where he/she lives, people he/she knows and things he/she has. Can interact in a simple way provided the other person talks slowly and clearly and is prepared to help.